THE ASTONISHING YOUTH

BOOKS BY THE SAME AUTHOR

Methodist History

> Family Circle (a study of the Epworth Household)
> John Wesley and the Eighteenth Century
> After Wesley
> Methodism and England
> This Methodism
> Adam Clarke
> S. E. Keeble: Pioneer and Prophet

Social Studies

> One Increasing Purpose (Beckly Lecture, 1947)
> Church and Society
> The Signs of our Times (Cato Lecture, 1957)

JOHN WESLEY: 1703-91

THE ASTONISHING YOUTH

*A Study of John Wesley
as Men Saw Him*

by
MALDWYN EDWARDS

'He is an astonishing youth and may be saluted
like the Eastern Monarchs, "O King, live for ever".'
(Charles Wesley in a letter to his wife, June 1758)

WIPF & STOCK · Eugene, Oregon

Wipf and Stock Publishers
199 W 8th Ave, Suite 3
Eugene, OR 97401

The Astonishing Youth
A Study of John Wesley as Men Saw Him
By Edwards, Maldwyn
Copyright©1959 Methodist Publishing - Epworth Press
ISBN 13: 978-194982-0494-1
Publication date 9/10/2014
Previously published by Epworth Press, 1959

"Every effort has been made to trace the current copyright
owner of this publication but without success. If you have any
information or interest in the copyright, please contact the publishers."

**FOR
BRIAN**

ACKNOWLEDGEMENTS

I wish to record my gratitude to Mrs Pierce Jones for typing my manuscript, and to my daughter, Miss Carol Edwards, B.A., for preparing the Index. M. E.

CONTENTS

JOHN WESLEY . . . . FRONTISPIECE

ACKNOWLEDGEMENTS 6

NOTE ON BOOKS 9

INTRODUCTION 11

1 THE CRITICS AND THE CONTROVERSIALISTS . 19

2 THE TESTIMONY OF HIS FAMILY AND FRIENDS 33

3 WHY HE WAS LOVED 61

4 THE DECADES OF HIS MINISTRY . . . 85

5 THE FINAL ANALYSIS 111

INDEX 127

NOTE ON BOOKS

Journal—*The Journal of John Wesley*, 8 vols, Standard Edition (London, 1909).

Letters—*The Letters of John Wesley*, 8 vols, Standard Edition (London, 1931).

Works—*The Works of John Wesley*, 14 vols, 3rd Edition (London, 1829-31).

In *Journal* references I have given the date when that seemed especially indicated.

INTRODUCTION

THIS ESSAY MUST not be looked upon as yet another life of John Wesley. It is rather an endeavour—and as I should like to think the first endeavour—to see Wesley as his contemporaries saw him; to see him not as the instrument of a great revival but as a man; to see him not as a heroic figure of the past, but as he appeared to his family, his friends, his critics, and indeed his enemies.

We know of John Wesley as 'the greatest figure in eighteenth-century England', 'one of the world's greatest religious leaders', and by many such tributes to his enduring fame and influence. These expressions relieve our feelings, even if they cannot describe adequately his immense hold on the imagination and life of men; but one consequence of such hyperbole is that John Wesley the man may escape us. To great numbers he remains a solitary, austere and even unattractive figure. It is astonishing for example to read in the *Oxford Dictionary of the Christian Church* that John's brother, Charles Wesley, was 'a more gentle and attractive character' (p. 1446), and even more amazing that the paragraph on Charles Wesley describes him as a 'more balanced and livelier character than his brother'. No words could be more inaptly chosen. Charles was essentially lovable, but in his quick temper and his rapid moods of gaiety and depression he was hardly to be described as balanced. John, on the other hand, was as imperturbable and even-tempered as his mother. Not even a vixenish and violently unstable wife could rouse him to anger; nothing remains either in his words or in his letters to her which does him discredit. It was his sanguine frame of mind and his easy and friendly disposition which made so deep an impression on his greatest biographer, Robert Southey. As for Charles being the livelier, it is enough to say in all gentleness, that he was subject to fits of depression which grew rather than diminished as the years went by. The robust encouragement, the spur to greater endeavour, came never from Charles to John but always from John to Charles. All who met John noted his liveliness; the longest ride under the worst conditions could not diminish his ardour or lower his spirits. By way of illustration I take one extract from his *Journal*, but examples could be multiplied indefinitely.

On 24th February 1748 he arrived at Holyhead, but he still had not sailed by 28th February, and on that day wrote:

'I never knew men make such poor, lame excuses as these captains did for not sailing. It put me in mind of the epigram:

> There are, if rightly I methink,
> Five causes why a man should drink;

which, with a little alteration, would just suit them:

INTRODUCTION

There are, unless my memory fail,
Five causes why we should not sail:
The fog is thick; the wind is high;
It rains; or may do by-and-by;
Or—any other reason why.'[1]

Call John any name, but as you value your reputation for fairness do not call him dull. His liveliness not only sustained him through his incredible journeyings on English roads for fifty years but quickened the zeal of countless others. The rise of the Methodist Societies is in itself a sure evidence of an essential liveliness!

But if an authoritative dictionary, so justly praised, can make such egregious misstatements about John Wesley's disposition, how can the wayfaring man be expected not to stumble? There obviously is abroad a totally erroneous impression of a great leader who was remote and even unbalanced. It is high time to recapture the true Wesley, a leader but a friend, disciplined but attractive, single-minded but sociable—for this is the Wesley who emerges from a study of his own writings and from the evidence of his contemporaries. Let no one call it an idealized picture, an Oliver Cromwell without his warts; to remain invincibly critical and assert that it is too good to be true is to defy the facts. The truth is that a new portrait is long overdue. The real

[1] *Journal*, III.335.

THE ASTONISHING YOUTH

Wesley must be allowed to emerge from the concealing mists of popular misunderstanding and prejudice.

In a most unusual degree John Wesley possessed two qualities that are not commonly linked. He had both strength and sweetness, and therefore he possessed both authority and charm; men could respect him as a leader and love him as a man. It might well be said of him, to adapt the words which Julius Caesar wrote in another context, that in his contact with people, 'he came, he saw, he conquered'.

This book, then, is a portrait of the man or perhaps more precisely a portrait of the inner man; not of John Wesley evangelist, reformer and Church builder, but of Wesley in himself. It is a tribute to one who was gay and lovable, one who fulfilled his own dictum in his own life by being 'the friend of all and the enemy of none'.

If any further clue is needed to the man we shall discover, it may be found in the words written of him by Mrs Charles Wesley in the preface which she wrote to a volume of her husband's sermons:

'The character of the brothers was distinctly different. John was born with a temper which scarcely any injuries could provoke, ingratitude ruffle, or contradictions weary. This disposition peculiarly qualified him to govern: but he was so far from arrogating authority or demanding submission, and his gentleness and forbearance rendered him so much the object of love amongst the people who placed themselves under his care that they considered "their sovereign pastor as a sovereign good"....

'The peculiar virtue of John was forgiveness of enemies. He has been frequently known to receive into his confidence those who had betrayed it and basely injured him. They not only subsisted on his bounty but shared his affection; nor was it easy to convince him that any had deceived him; or if it were attested by facts he would only allow it had been so in that single instance.' My thesis is that Wesley exercised authority and yet inspired affection.

THE CRITICS AND THE CONTROVERSIALISTS

CHAPTER ONE

THE CRITICS AND THE CONTROVERSIALISTS

ONCE A MAN'S greatness is acknowledged a further question remains to tease the mind. Was he lonely and forbidding as any high mountain peak or had he still the human touch? A man's very gifts and powers of leadership may serve to separate him from his fellows. He may then be respected and even admired, but he will not be loved. John Wesley was not of that company. He had the power of winning peoples' affection as well as their respect. He was likeable—essentially likeable. He led an army who chose to follow because they accepted the man as well as the message. For them, as Crabbe said:

> *John the Elder*
> *Was the John Divine.*

Upon his death the *Gentleman's Magazine* justly remarked that 'he was one of the few characters who outlived enmity and prejudices and received in his later years every mark of esteem from every denomination'.[1]

This did not imply that all who met him accepted

[1] See *Gentleman's Magazine*, Vol. LXI (1791), pp. 282-4, for the full encomium.

his authority. He became the undisputed head of the Holy Club when he returned from his curacy at Wroote in 1729, but in time Benjamin Ingham who had sailed to Georgia with him left him to become a Moravian minister. John Gambold, his entirely lovable but impractical friend, and Stonehouse, the convert of Charles Wesley, also joined the Moravian Church. Scarcely any of that original band of brothers shared Wesley's views as the years went by.

The excellent James Hervey, who had remained on friendly terms with him, was grievously hurt toward the end of his life by Wesley's criticism of his *Theron and Aspasio*. 'Wesley', he said in a publication produced posthumously, had spoken 'with the solemnity of a censor and the authority of a dictator.'[2] When John Wesley came to reply he carefully answered the twelve charges against him, but he would not do other than speak in love and admiration of the author himself.[3] 'Shall my hand be upon that saint of God? No; let him rest in Abraham's bosom. When my warfare is accomplished, may I rest with him till the resurrection of the just!'[4] Perhaps this isolated example of a life-long friend turning upon him may have been due to the fact that Hervey's attack was 'edited' by the unkindly disposed William Cudworth, who was given permission to 'put out and put in' what he pleased. Certainly in all the other cases the

[2] *The Scriptural Doctrine of Imputed Righteousness Defended.*
[3] 'Preface to a Treatise on Justification', *Works*, X.316-46.
[4] Ibid. p. 337.

drifting away from the original leader may just as well be interpreted as his departure from them. But were they not all at a stage when their careers and convictions had yet to be determined?

More important is the charge that in his own Methodist society some of his close helpers sickened of his authority and went their several ways. This is another indictment which will not bear close scrutiny. When John Wesley quoted a sentence of Hervey's, 'Believers who are notorious transgressors in themselves, have a sinless obedience in Christ', he commented aptly: 'O syren song! Pleasing sound to James Wheatley, Thomas Williams, James Relly.'[5] He might well have added the name of his own brother-in-law the infamous Westley Hall. Others who left were men of mental instability or marked eccentricity of conduct. Thomas Maxfield was the young man whom Mrs Susanna Wesley heard to such profit that she counselled her son not to prevent him from preaching at the Foundery: 'I charge you before God, beware what you do; for Thomas Maxfield is as much called to preach the Gospel as ever you were!' Wesley sensibly listened to her advice and waived aside his former prejudices. 'It is the Lord's doing,' he said, 'let Him do what seemeth good. What am I, that I should withstand God?' He accepted him as a lay preacher and within a year (1740) had appointed twenty others. Nevertheless Wesley later had to

[5] *Works*, X.326. All men who started well but later failed.

THE ASTONISHING YOUTH

record in his *Journal* that Maxfield was stirring up disaffection against him.[6] When he refused to preach at the Foundery and flouted Wesley's authority, the gulf was unbridgeable. He took with him 106 members and settled down independently to preach an uncompromising Calvinism.[7] In 1778 he joined with other Calvinist critics of John Wesley in adding his own vituperative pamphlet to the hailstorm of invective in which John Wesley was deluged.[8] John Wesley replied most temperately in an open letter, and despite the intransigence of his opponent was ready to sign himself; 'Your still affectionate brother.' The overture was not accepted, but five years later Wesley recorded in his Journal that he visisted 'Mr Maxfield struck with a violent stroke of palsy. He was senseless and seemed near death; but we besought God for him, and his spirit revived, I cannot but think in answer to prayer.'[9] Some weeks later he preached at Mr Maxfield's chapel and reported: 'Prejudice seems now dying away: God grant it may never revive.' To the end Wesley strove to repair a breach which he himself had never made.

John Cennick, hymn-writer and composer of our best-known family Graces, appointed by Wesley to Kingswood, was another early follower whose defiant Calvinism and head-strong behaviour made it impossible for him to remain. When he separated, half

[6] 28th April 1763.   [7] Ibid. 18th November 1763.
[8] The 'storm' was at its height during 1777 to 1779.
[9] 21st December 1782.

the society went with him.[10] Almost twenty years later (12th October 1760) John Wesley, when visiting the classes at Kingswood, had to record that there was no increase, and to lament that 'the weak man John Cennick confounded the poor people with strange doctrines'. After five years as a Calvinist and a professed follower of Whitefield, Cennick became a Moravian and spent some time preaching and labouring in Germany. He can hardly be quoted as a stable leader who found Wesley's rule intolerable. He was rather a well meaning but unstable man who left Methodism because he disagreed with its tenets.

Last of the better-known men who left Wesley was John Bennet, who, helped by Charles Wesley, married the woman to whom John Wesley had considered himself morally affianced. But John Wesley, after the first shock of sorrow and surprise, did not allow the loss of Grace Murray to affect his relations with Bennet. At his first meeting with him after his marriage, and in the presence of Whitefield, John Nelson and his brother Charles, John Wesley kissed him and accepted with astonishing calm what he believed to be God's will. Despite a magnanimity of spirit which allowed Wesley to visit Rochdale a fortnight later at Bennet's invitation, the younger man showed a strange churlishness. He requited kindness with treachery and denounced Wesley as a teacher of Popish doctrines. When Wesley heard it he only

[10] *Journal*, 7th and 8th March 1741.

THE ASTONISHING YOUTH

remarked in his *Journal:* 'Lord, lay not this sin to his charge.'[11] Despite Wesley's irenic attitude, Bennet continued in his violent suspicions. When he died in 1759 as the pastor of a Calvinistic church in Warrington, he had rejected both Wesley the man and his teaching. But here also was evidence of a man at the mercy of his own sullen temperament. His defection cannot be set to Wesley's account.

Other seceders there were, such as fanatical George Bell who believed that the world would end on 28th February 1763 and who until 1st March of that year remained in that conviction 'as unmoved as a rock'. Their adherence or secession would prove nothing.

There remain the controversialists. But it is fair to say that when men are obstinately sure of themselves, and when their convictions are prejudices, they are not likely to be careful of an opponent's person or his beliefs. The eighteenth century in any case was remarkable for a bold coarseness of language which reached its height in controversy. Just as the satirists, Hogarth, Gillray, and Rowlandson achieved their objective by gross exaggeration, so writers flayed their victims with merciless invective. Even Burke could speak of Chatham as 'the grand artificer of fraud' and a clergyman could declare Archbishop Tillotson to be 'a traitor who sold his Lord for a better price than Judas had done'.[12]

[11] *Journal,* 26th March 1752.
[12] *Wesley's England,* J. H. Whiteley, p. 291.

THE CRITICS AND THE CONTROVERSIALISTS

Smollett in his *History of England* spoke of Methodism as 'an imposture', as 'fanaticism and superstition', and unhappily for himself described Whitefield and the two Wesleys as a 'few obscure preachers'. Likewise Horace Walpole, in an ignorance only less complete because he went once to hear John Wesley, described him as clever an actor as Garrick. Such attacks could not possibly injure Wesley's reputation then or now.

More serious was the attack of other Christians. If he had charm they seemed singularly oblivious to it. This however was partly because they never knew him as a man; they judged him by his opinions, and even those were often misunderstood. Such men as Potter, Archbishop of Canterbury, and Gibson, Bishop of London, were critical of Wesley's views, but they knew him and they never spoke ill of his person. Bishop Gibson's Pastoral Letter of 1739 attacking 'lukewarmness on the one hand and enthusiasm on the other' was directed against Whitefield, and it was Whitefield who replied to it. Just before his death in 1748 the churchwardens of St Bartholomew the Great appealed to Dr Gibson to over-ride the action of their rector who had opened his pulpit to John Wesley. He refused. 'What would you have me do?' he said. 'I have no right to hinder him. Mr Wesley is a clergyman regularly ordained and under no ecclesiastical censure.'

The two prelates who attacked John Wesley with

venom were those who knew least about him. According to his biographer Bishop Hurd, William Warburton, Bishop of Gloucester, gained his knowledge of Wesley and his views from the *Journal,* and on that slender foundation wrote his *Office and Operations of the Holy Spirit.* Wesley, in his 'Letter', replied fully to the various charges.[13] They amounted in substance to the accusation that he claimed 'almost every apostolic gift in as full and ample a manner as they were possessed of old'. It was ironic that Warburton should attack Wesley's presumptuousness when he himself was known as pugnacious and arrogant. He was whipped so soundly for this by Bishop Lowth in a cleverly sarcastic pamphlet that Wesley who relished the dextrous use of a verbal rapier commented; 'If anything human could be a cure for pride surely such a medicine as this would!'

More important than Warburton's feeble sally was the extensive argument of George Lavington, Bishop of Exeter, that John Wesley was a Papist in disguise.[14] The bishop had compared certain selections from the visions and sayings of eminent Roman Catholics with extracts from the journals and writings of Whitefield and Wesley. The charge of course was monstrous, but Wesley convicted the bishop not only of woeful

[13] For the full title and contents, see *Works,* IX.117-73.
[14] The work was entitled *Enthusiasm of Methodists and Papists Compared* and it was published in three parts between 1749 and 1757. Later it appeared in two volumes. Wesley's unanswerable reply entitled *Letters to the Bishop of Exeter* can be found in *Works,* IX.1-64.

ignorance but of downright dishonesty in his manipulation of passages quoted from the *Journal* and in his divorcing of them from their context. Actually this best known and most widely read attack on an Anglican bishop had a pleasant conclusion. In 1762 Wesley was at Exeter and attended Holy Communion at the cathedral. He wrote in his *Journal* (29th August 1762): 'I was pleased to partake of the Lord's Supper with my old opponent Bishop Lavington and may we sit down together in the kingdom of our Father.' A few weeks later the bishop had died. Despite his attack on Wesley, his own diocese covering the whole of Cornwall showed the greatest increase in Methodist membership.

These Anglican critics were mild in language compared with his Calvinistic opponents, especially Augustus Toplady, Rowland and Richard Hill. When religious bigotry lent a cutting edge to slander the lowest depths of scurrility were eagerly plumbed. In the seventies Wesley was continually being daubed with every species of verbal filth, and the befouling reached its height as the decade came to its close. The chief offender was Augustus Toplady, author of the deathless hymn, 'Rock of Ages'. He addressed a pamphlet to Wesley with the title: *An Old Fox Tarr'd and Feathered*' (1775). In a longer work he wrote in the advertisement: 'I foresee one objection in particular to which the ensuing work is liable, viz. that the two Pelagian Methodists namely Mr John Wesley and

Mr Walter Sellon whose fraudulent perversions of truth, facts, and common sense, gave the first occasion to the present undertaking, are not persons of sufficient consequence to merit so large and explicit a refutation.'[15] Small wonder that he said: 'Mr John Wesley is the only opponent I ever had whom I chastized with a studious disregard to ceremony.'[16] Rowland Hill was, if possible, more offensive and intemperate still. He described Wesley as 'a venal profligate—an apostate miscreant, a wicked slanderer'. In a pamphlet written in 1777 he further accused him of 'calumniating the living, traducing the dead, and palming barefaced falsehoods on the world'.[17]

These attacks, however, did not reflect adversely upon John Wesley but upon their authors. Indeed the one pleasant feature of so unsavoury a decade in religious controversy is the way Wesley dealt with his traducers. Replying to Toplady's doctrine rather than his calumnies, Wesley said that in sum it amounted to the fact that 'one in twenty, suppose of mankind are elected; nineteen in twenty are reprobated. The elect shall be saved, do what they will. The reprobate shall be damned do what they can.'[18] Replying fully but temperately to a work of Rowland Hill's, he con-

[15] *Historic Proof of the Doctrinal Calvinism of the Church of England*, 2 vols (1774).
[16] Postscript to *A Caveat Against Unsound Doctrines* (1770).
[17] For the pamphlets written by Toplady and Hill, see *Anti-Methodist Publications*, Richard Green (1902).
[18] *Works*, X.370.

cluded: 'Sir I love you still; though I cannot esteem you as I did once.'[19] In a second reply to a further attack, he besought Rowland Hill 'to resume the scholar, the gentleman, and the Christian'.[20]

The appeal went unheeded, but at least Wesley refused to go down with his opponents to a verbal garbage heap. He answered their splenetic attacks in a mood of candour but of courtesy. Charles Wesley, referring to his brother, told James Hutton (17th October 1773): 'I never yet heard him speak one unkind word of Mr Hill or Mr Toplady.' This magnanimity was well illustrated in John Wesley's wordy duel with the witty Father O'Leary. Wesley had written a letter to the *Public Advertiser* which was reprinted in the *Protestant Magazine*. Father O'Leary vigorously replied in six letters which were reprinted under one title.[21] This in turn provoked Wesley to reply in two letters addressed to *Freemen's Journal*. The keen satire and wit of O'Leary puzzled John Wesley not a little. He complained of this 'poetry talk', this 'artful endeavour', and most revealing phrase of all, 'this throwing dust in the eyes of honest Englishmen'. Plainly he was puzzled as well as pained by his nimble antagonist. This being so, it is all the more pleasant to recall that when Wesley visited Dublin seven years later he seized promptly an invitation to have breakfast with O'Leary. He

[19] Ibid. p. 414.   [20] Ibid. p. 454.
[21] *Mr O'Leary's Remarks on the Rev. Mr W.'s Letters in Defence of the Protestant Association in England* (London, 1779).

records in his *Journal*, 12th May 1787: 'I was not at all displeased at being disappointed. He is not the stiff queer man that I expected, but of an easy genteel carriage and seems not to be wanting either in sense or learning.'

This comment, written only four years before his death, may show fittingly a man who did not allow keen and often personal attacks to warp his judgement or embitter his relations with his opponents. He was courteous in reply and always ready to be friendly. When his critics fought him from a distance they could sustain their invective, but when they actually came to know him, they might, like George Whitefield, maintain their separate views, but they could not maintain their anger.

THE TESTIMONY OF HIS FAMILY
AND FRIENDS

CHAPTER TWO

THE TESTIMONY OF HIS FAMILY AND FRIENDS

IT IS NOT possible to avoid using that much-abused word 'charm' to describe the effect of John Wesley on people. If 'even the ranks of Tuscany could scarce forbear to cheer', the rest were willing victims. They must often have regarded Wesley's critics as Philistines in Matthew Arnold's use of that word—'strong dogged unenlightened opponents of the chosen people, of the children of light'.[1] A severe test of a man's essential nature is how he appears to the members of his own family. Give all possible respect to the Haworth Parsonage, and the Epworth Rectory has still its own impregnable place in the history of the world. No such remarkable group of parents, brothers and sisters ever lived under a family roof. Despite his short temper, his bad farming, his undue pre-occupation with his *Dissertations on Job*, and his wrong treatment of Hetty, the Rector was a great and good man. When he came to Epworth at the close of the seventeenth century (1697) he found a peasantry as sullen and intractable as their own countryside. On at least two occasions they may have been

[1] *Essays in Criticism.*

responsible for setting fire to the old Parsonage and once they maimed his cattle. Even some of the gentry were opposed to him on political grounds, and for a short time secured his imprisonment for debt.[2] There was no moaning and certainly no cry for mercy. By dogged service to his parishioners and through the tactful help of his wife, Samuel Wesley gradually won their respect and liking. In a letter to his eldest son (28th February 1733) he wrote that when he began there were twenty and now there were above a hundred at the Communion Service. When John Wesley preached on his father's tombstone in 1742 and saw a 'vast multitude gathered from all parts', he thought of his father's forty years of service to Epworth and commented: 'Let none think his labour of love is lost because the fruit does not immediately appear.' He said that the seed sown so long since had now sprung up, 'bringing forth repentance and remission of sins'.

A man who had wrestled with so many giants and who was a bonny fighter to the end was not likely to be mistaken in the calibre of his son. He knew John's logical cast of mind, and warned him that though he thought everything could be carried by dint of argument, he would find by and by 'how very little is done in the world by clear reason'. In another letter to John (1725) he confessed his admiration of his reasoning powers, but added cautiously: 'He that believes and yet argues against reason is half a Papist or enthusiast.

[2] See my *Family Circle*, pp. 18-20.

He that would make revelation bend to his own shallow reason is either half a deist or a lunatic. O my dear! steer clear between this Scylla and Charybdis.'

Many of his letters were concerned with John's studies, but in a notable letter (1st December 1730) written both to John and Charles and strongly approving their mode of life at Oxford, he concluded: 'I hear my son, John, has the honour of being styled "the Father of the Holy Club": if it be so, I must be the grandfather of it; and I need not say that I had rather any of my sons should be so dignified and distinguished than to have the title of His Holiness.'

There were only two occasions when the Rector showed the smallest sense of displeasure with John. One was his son's refusal to accept the living at Epworth when age and infirmity compelled him to think of retirement. He accepted John's reasons for refusal, and allowed no breach to form, but he did not really understand them. In the second instance, the beautiful and gifted Hetty Wesley had most grievously wounded Samuel and Susanna by eloping with her suitor to Lincoln. When it was clear he did not intend marriage immediately, she returned home. But the harm was done, and the Rector accepted Hetty's declaration that she would marry the first man who asked her. He turned out to be William Wright, a travelling plumber and glazier from Louth. On every score of breeding, education and temperament he was a totally unsuitable match, but the Rector held her to her promise. Even after her unhappy marriage neither the Rector nor Susanna would relent. John argued many times with his father on behalf of Hetty. Finally he took the bold step of preaching in his parents' presence at Wroote (Sunday 28th August 1726) on 'The Universal Charity or the Charity due to Wicked Persons'. With great plainness and courage he enlarged on the Christian virtues of magnanimity and forgiveness. His mother said, 'You writ this sermon for Hetty,' and through Charles, the Rector let John know how deeply hurt he was. This was the only occasion in their lives when a definite difference caused sore feelings. John did not withdraw his opinions nor seek to excuse them, but he told his father he would not willingly cause him any pain nor did he intend any unfilial conduct. He volunteered to act as amanuensis for his father and his offer was accepted 'with tears of joy'. When he came to die it was to John he said those words which foreshadowed the Methodist teaching on Assurance: 'The inward witness, son, the inward witness; that is the proof, the strongest proof of Christianity.'[3]

The relationship of Susanna and her son is known to the world. Did she not write a special letter about the Rectory fire of 1709 in which she dwelt upon the providential escape of her son John?[4] Henceforward

[3] John Wesley quoted this saying in a letter to John Smith (Archbishop Secker?), 22nd March 1748.
[4] *Works*, XIII.517-18.

she was sure he had a special work to do. The part of Thursday night that she gave to him made so permanent an impression that he wrote in later life that if only she could still give it, he had no doubt it would correct his heart, as in those days it formed his judgement. Her letters to John are mainly concerned with his spiritual development,[5] but occasionally a more personal note creeps in. In a letter dated 25th October 1732 she was concerned about his health and said: 'Unless you take more care than you do, you will put the matter past dispute in a little time.'

Devoted as she was to Sammy her eldest son, she was, for all her independence of mind, quickly brought over to the new evangelical teachings of John and Charles. Sammy was amazed and distressed. In a letter written to his mother in October 1739 he confessed: 'It was with exceeding concern and grief I heard you had countenanced a spreading delusion so far as to be one of Jack's congregation. Is it not enough that I am bereft of both my brothers, but must my mother follow too? I earnestly beseech the Almighty to preserve you from joining a schism at the close of your life. . . . they boast of you already as a disciple.' Despite this protest from a son so soon to die, Susanna was not to be moved. She spent her last years at the Foundery and took part in its services. When she died (30th July 1742) her children, as she had requested, sang a hymn of

[5] See *Family Circle*, pp. 76-7.

praise to God. In what was to be counted a Methodist tradition she entered heaven with a shout of praise.

The parents' admiration and love of John was shared by brothers and sisters. Sammy at the very close of his life was shaken by news of the Methodist revival, but his love for John never wavered throughout his life. He had given John advice when he was at Charterhouse and later at Christ Church. Even when John was made Fellow of Lincoln College he still sent occasional sermons to Sammy for criticism. In the letters about the succession to the Epworth living John wrote to his elder brother on equal terms, and at Savannah[6] his tone is almost that of a teacher. By the time of the Revival's opening, therefore, Sammy had no delusions about his inability to change John's mind or alter his course. He said in his last letter to John (3rd September 1739) that he did not fear that the Church would excommunicate John but that John would excommunicate the Church. His tone was milder than in previous letters and the mood had changed to puzzlement rather than criticism. John was congratulated on the building of a Charity School and Sammy wished a church might be built for the colliers. The letter ended with expressions of love. Whether John Wesley would have won over his elder brother we shall never know, because two months later Sammy was dead. John arrived at Tiverton on

[6] 23rd November 1736.

21st November 1739 and heard that 'several days before my brother went hence, God had given him a calm and full assurance of his interest in Christ. O may everyone who opposes it be thus convinced that this doctrine is of God.' The words would suggest that the one who had been with Sammy 'in all his weakness' was convinced that before he died his antipathy to the Revival had vanished. This was certainly the impression John received.

Apart from this one possible exception, all the remaining family not only were susceptible to John's charm but accepted his evangelical views. Mary had died in childbirth one year after her marriage to John Whitelamb, the curate of Wroote.[7] The Revival was still four years away, so one can only say that with the rest of her sisters she idolized her brother. Writing to him often, she begged him to keep writing to her, because 'your letters give so much satisfaction to your loving sister'. Kezzy (Kezziah) was nearest in age to Charles and the two were always specially drawn to each other. Yet it was Kezzy who told John she loved him 'with more than sister's love'. When at one period he had not replied for some time to her letter, she begged him not to treat her affection lightly and remarked, 'love is a present for a mighty king'. Like her sister Mary, Kezzy died early.[8] The brothers were only in the opening years of their

---

[7] 1st November 1734. For her story see *Family Circle*, pp. 142-5.
[8] In 1740 at the age of 30 years.

campaigning, but Kezzy shared their joy. A *Journal* entry (Thursday 5th October 1738) records that whilst Charles went 'shamefully unwilling' to visit the prisoners at Newgate, John and a few friends went down the river, 'reading' and 'singing' as they sailed. At Blendon they were joined by Kezzy; John and she had a talk together, and at 4 p.m. they set out singing, with William Delamotte as companion, for an hour and a half. Then it was time for Wesley to return for a Society meeting and the happy party broke up. Later entries speak of him on many occasions walking with Kezzy and having tea with her. There can be no question that Kezzy had no reservations about her brother John nor about the movement he was leading.

Of Anne (Nancy) we know less than any, but she alone seems to have had a happy marriage. About 1725 she married John Lambert, a land surveyor, highly intelligent and respected. In the early days of the Revival her brother sometimes called upon her, and on 1st January 1742 when he was in a high fever and confined to bed at the Foundery, sister Anne was present. Wesley, who could not allow a high temperature to keep him idle, summoned the Bands to meet in his room. Afterwards with some misgiving he turned to Anne and asked if she was offended. 'Offended!' she said, 'I wish I could always be with you. I thought I was in heaven.'

But it is the remaining sisters who cannot be omitted

from any story of John Wesley.[9] Emilia (Emily), the eldest sister, would almost have desired a proprietary interest in John. When she was in the midst of an unhappy love affair she begged him to be the repository of her secrets, and in a letter written four years later[10] she declared 'full well you know that even from our childhood you have been selected from all our numerous family for my intimate companion, my counsellor in difficulties, the dear partner of my joys and griefs'. When after her unhappy marriage to Harper, the Epworth apothecary, she left him and came to live in a room at the Foundery, she entered into all its ministries. Later when West Street Chapel was taken, John maintained her in the Chapel House. She continued to attend the services and share the life of the Society until she died there in great peace in the year 1771.

Those who picture Wesley as the lonely leader might well consider that Emily was with him in London until 1771, and in that same year Charles moved from Bristol to make his permanent home in London. Nor was this all. Hetty lived in London after her marriage until her death in 1750. She became a Methodist and attended services in the Foundery. John and Charles paid her occasional visits. For some years she was in bodily weakness, and when

---

[9] I have not mentioned 'Sukey', who married the drunken Dick Ellison and some years after left him to live in London. She plays no special part in the Wesley story.

[10] 31st December 1729.

THE ASTONISHING YOUTH

she came to die she said to a friend: 'You know we Methodists always die in a transport of joy.'

Beyond question Martha was John Wesley's favourite sister. In old age she confessed to Adam Clarke that when she was a girl and the rest of the family desired to test her 'philosophic steadiness', it was brother John who always took her part. When he was at Oxford in 1727 she wrote confessing the desire to have first place in his esteem. 'I believe I need not tell you that when we love any person very well we desire to be loved by them in the same degree, and though I cannot possibly be so vain as to think that I do for my own personal merits deserve more love than my sisters, yet can you blame me if I sometimes wish I had been so happy as to have had the first place in your heart?'[11]

When her wretchedly unhappy union with the polygamous Westley Hall was over, she was able freely to devote her time to Sally Wesley, Charles's daughter and her own intimate and beloved companion. It was Sally who was with her when she died. She also had her literary interests. She was friendly with Dr Johnson, and on the very day (15th April 1781) when John Wesley was in danger of death vainly attempting to cross to Ireland in a violent storm, Martha Hall was dining with Dr Johnson and discussing resurrections, apparitions, and voices of the dead. Boswell recorded in *The Life* that Mrs

[11] Written from Wroote, 7th February 1727.

Hall resembled her famous brother John both in figure and manner, and he added, 'lean, lank, preaching Mrs Hall was exquisite'.

Her chief interest, however, lay in the Methodist work in London, where in those days Charles had his home and John his headquarters. Like her brother she kept her sprightliness even in old age. When she was seventy-eight years old John wrote her: 'There is hardly a father in England that can furnish three persons who, after so many years, are so young as my brother, and you, and me.'[12] But once John Wesley died she suddenly felt old. Four months after his death she followed him, and was buried in the same vault in Wesley's Chapel, City Road. So it was that the two who were so united in their lives were not divided in death.

Of all the family, however, it is John and Charles who are imperishably linked together. This is not solely because one was the architect and the other 'the sweet singer' of the Revival. Each was necessary to the movement, and despite their differences each was necessary to the other. Charles gave their relationship a rude jolt when he intervened so hastily in John's only real love affair, and during his brother's absence married the bewildered and vacillating Grace Murray to her other suitor John Bennet. John took care not to consult his brother before he ran into an unfortunate marriage with Mrs Vazeille. It was an

[12] *Journal*, VI.318, note 3.

abiding disappointment to John when, after ten years of joint campaigning in itinerant open-air preaching and the formation of Methodist societies, Charles came to Bristol after his marriage and settled down to the joys and sorrows of family life.[13] After a further few years in which from time to time he was at his brother's disposal, he limited himself to the work in Bristol. His *Journal* ends with an itinerary in 1756 which, lasting from 17th September to 6th November, took him through the North and the Midlands back to Bristol. In 1771 he moved with his family to London. The house in Bristol had long since proved too small and he was needed often in the metropolis. In 1766 John Wesley had re-echoed an old complaint; '... are we not jointly engaged in such a work as probably no two other men on earth are? Why then do we keep at such a distance? ... Let us make the full use of the little time that remains.' Once in London Charles Wesley gave himself with entire devotion to the care of the Methodist Societies.

Perhaps John, in his desire to have his brother on the road, never fully realized what it meant to have his brother first at the Methodist headquarters in the West and then for seventeen years in London. Writing to James Hutton, Charles Wesley made clear where his heart lay: 'I am fixed, resolved, determined, sworn

[13] He married Sarah Gwynne, daughter of a wealthy Welsh squire, on 8th April 1749, and they took up residence in Bristol on 1st September.

to stand by the Methodists and my Brother, through thick and thin . . .' By his hymn-writing, his preaching, his administration of the Sacrament of the Lord's Supper, and his counsels to John, he loyally fulfilled that intention.

If John had misgivings about Charles, it was certainly true that Charles became increasingly troubled about John's actions and the inevitable separation from the Anglican Church which they foreshadowed. The essential difference between the brothers was that Charles was a Methodist Churchman; his Methodism was adjectival to the Church of England. Though John would emphatically have denied it, he was an Anglican Methodist. Charles Wesley himself had summed up their different attitudes with shrewdness: 'All the difference between my brother and me was that my brother's first object was the Methodists and then the Church: mine was first the Church and then the Methodists.'[14] In the words of Dr Beaumont, John Wesley was like a skilful rower who keeps his eyes on the shore whilst every stroke of his oars takes him farther away. Nothing could deflect him in his intention to save souls. Charles was shocked at the licensing of the Preaching Houses (1787). The legal adviser, Mr Clulow, had convinced John that 'it was the safest way to license all our chapels and all our travelling preachers . . . and that no Justice or bench of Justices has any authority to refuse licensing either

[14] See *Letters*, VIII.267.

the house or the preachers'.[15] It was the third blow to fall in rapid succession. John Wesley had formed the Conference into a legal body formed of a hundred preachers nominated by himself in his 'Deed of Declaration' (28th February 1784); this gave Methodism an independent legal status. Then, before Charles had recovered from the shock, brother John went a long step farther. After the War of American Independence the Anglican clergy in America had either fled to Canada or had been made to feel unwanted. The action of the mother country had made their own position intolerable. It was estimated that eighteen thousand Methodists were deprived of the Sacraments. In such an emergency, and fortified by his belief that he was 'a Scriptural $\dot{\epsilon}\pi\iota\sigma\kappa\sigma\pi\sigma s$ as much as any man in England or in Europe',[16] he set Dr Coke apart as Superintendent of Methodism in America with instructions to ordain Francis Asbury as his fellow Superintendent.[17] Lord Mansfield had said that ordination was separation and the horrified Charles Wesley had no doubt that he was right. Where would all this lead? But John had no second thoughts. 'I must and will', he said, 'save as many souls as I can while I live without being careful about what may possibly be when I die.'[18]

[15] *Journal*, 3rd November 1787.
[16] *Letters*, VII.284, 19th August 1785.
[17] 2nd September 1784. On the previous day he had ordained Whatcoat and Vasey for the work in America.
[18] *Letters*, VII.289, 13th September 1785.

But three such heavy blows, with all the difference of conviction implied, could not affect Charles's love and admiration of his brother. In spite of them all, he wrote to John: 'Let us agree to differ . . . keep your authority while you live.'[19] When John Wesley wrote his sermon on 'The Catholic Spirit' and he declared that in the light of a common love of God and all mankind, any points of dispute should stand aside and never come into sight, he provided his own illustration. In the light of their love for one another, John and Charles allowed no dispute to estrange them. Charles died on 29th March 1788, and a month later John apologized to his sister-in-law for 'troubling' her with so many letters. He said he could not help it because he found her and her family so much on his heart, both 'for your own sake and for the sake of my brother'. No anecdote bears re-telling more than the story of Wesley taking a service at Bolton a fortnight after his brother's death. He announced his brother's hymn on 'Wrestling Jacob', and broke down and wept openly as he came to the lines

> *My company before is gone,*
> *And I am left alone with Thee.*

No one knew John better, and no one loved him more than his brother, Charles Wesley.

[19] 9th April 1787.

THE ASTONISHING YOUTH

It would be an easy and pleasant task to pass from the tributes of John's family to those of his numerous friends. Rich and poor, old and young, male and female, delighted in his company. Some of them fall into well-defined groups. They include such evangelical clergymen as Grimshaw of Haworth, Berridge of Everton, Vincent Perronet, vicar of Shoreham in Kent, and most of all his 'designated successor' Fletcher of Madeley. In a second group were public figures such as John Howard the prison reformer, William Wilberforce, Dr Johnson, who said 'he could talk well on any subject', and Lord George Gordon, the eccentric and half crazed, whom Wesley helped during his imprisonment in the Tower. In a third group were friends outside his Methodist Society, like George Whitefield whose love no doctrinal differences could disturb, his 'old friend' Howell Harris the Welsh evangelist,[20] and Dr Byrom the hymn-writer and scholar, 'who was not ashamed of being known as the particular friend of Wesley'.[21]

Then came the women whom Wesley addressed with such artless simplicity. Since his passion for his work was only second to his passion for God, Mrs Wesley had no possible cause for jealousy. He took an innocent delight in their company. He wrote to them in affectionate terms, but he loved them in general and not in particular, and could only suffer

[20] *Journal*, 14th August 1772.
[21] *Life and Times of John Wesley*, Luke Tyerman, II.484. He died in 1763.

his wife's outbursts without any comprehension. Nevertheless, though he went unscathed,[22] Mrs Wesley was not wrong in supposing that his women friends were very conscious of the Wesley charm. There is an apt comment of James Hutton to Count Zinzendorf made in 1740. He said: 'The Wesleys are a snare to young women... all fall in love with them.' Whether he was writing to Sarah Ryan, Mary Bishop, Ann Bolton, Elizabeth Ritchie, Mary Bosanquet, or Lady Maxwell, his first concern was for their spiritual welfare. But though the letters were those of a spiritual counsellor, it is obvious that his women correspondents were drawn to him by ties of affection and a great respect.

Lastly came his own assistants in the work of the Revival. Some were itinerant and therefore supported by the Connexion, whilst others were 'local', supporting themselves and living in their own localities. Here if anywhere we may expect signs of chafing at reins drawn too tightly, a certain restiveness under a rule that was autocratic. Hampson in his *Life of Wesley* accused Wesley of being 'fond of power'. He asserted that in the last ten or fifteen years of his dominion he was the most absolute of monarchs. Hampson was particularly disgruntled, but Wesley was plainly conscious of a wave of criticism when he discussed at length in the closing address to the Leeds Conference

[22] The exceptions are the Georgia friendship with Sophia Hopkey and the episode of Grace Murray. Even in these cases the lover was inhibited by the other-worldliness of the seeker after God.

THE ASTONISHING YOUTH

1766 his undeniable power and the use he made of it.[23] Without carrying much conviction he called it a burden which he would willingly transfer to others. More impressively he said that since his preachers served him as 'sons in the Gospel', none could call his power 'the shackling of free-born Englishmen'.

John Nelson describes vividly in his *Journal* the impression Wesley made on those who first met him. 'As soon as he got upon the stand he stroked back his hair and turned his face toward where I stood and I thought fixed his eyes on me. His countenance struck such an awful dread upon me before I heard him speak that it made my heart beat like the pendulum of a clock, and when he did speak I thought his whole discourse was aimed at me. When he had done I said, "This man can tell the secrets of my heart".' On a second meeting John Wesley took his hand and bade him not to quench the spirit. Nelson said 'it was a blessed conference to me', and a life-long friendship began. When he had become a preacher he accompanied Wesley on a tour of Cornwall and recalled that one night at St Ives both had to lie down to sleep on the floor.

'One morning about three o'clock Mr Wesley turned over and finding me awake clapped me on one side saying, "Brother Nelson, let us be of good cheer: I have one whole side yet, for the skin is off

[23] *Works*, VIII.310-13.

but on one side".' This was a tour in which they were usually short of food as well as beds. One day after preaching at St Hilary Downs 'Mr Wesley stopped his horse to pick the blackberries, saying, "Brother Nelson, we ought to be thankful that there are plenty of blackberries; for this is the best country I ever saw for getting a stomach, but the worst that I ever saw for getting food. Do the people think we can live by preaching?"' When John Nelson was forced to be a soldier Wesley met him at Durham and greatly encouraged him by telling him to use his strange circumstances as fresh opportunities for preaching. He said God had work for him in every place and would in time break his bonds in sunder. Partly through Methodist insistence Nelson found release, and Wesley, meeting him at Osmotherly, rejoiced with him at his deliverance.

Joseph Cownley was another of the early preachers whose respect for Wesley deepened into affection.[24] As with all the preachers, he carried to John Wesley his troubles and more especially his violent headaches. Wesley replied with great sympathy, and in one letter advised him not to take more labour than he could bear: 'Do as much as you can and no more.'

A third illustration of Wesley's hold over his preachers may be taken from Thomas Olivers' sense of gratitude for one whom he always called his

[24] *The Lives of Early Methodist Preachers*, II.19.

father.[25] When Wesley died he wrote a lengthy elegy in which he indicated the human qualities of one who was often misunderstood by those without intimate knowledge of him. Some of these verses may be chosen to light up the impression Wesley made on a preacher who was also for long years his Book Steward, and who therefore could judge him well.

The man I loved, the man by thousands prized,
By angels honour'd, but by fools despised,
Hath closed his eyes in death, and left me here in pain,
To sigh, and mourn, and weep, while life and love remain.

With pensive ears he heard the aged moan,
And saw their tears, and mix'd them with his own;
Then stretch'd his liberal hand, and shared his frugal store
And gave them all he could, and wish'd to give them more. . . .

When feuds and contests rose to wound our peace,
His prudence soon prevail'd to make them cease.
He heard our sad complaints; then look'd, and sweetly smiled:
We blush'd, and then shook hands, and so were reconciled. . . .

When'er we stray'd, by sin and error led,
He sought, and found us out, wherever fled;

[25] *The Lives of Early Methodist Preachers*, II.94.

Then kindly call'd us back, and spread his arms abroad,
To help our weakness home to happiness and God. . . .

For this his cheerful feet pursued their way,
Through winter's nights, and summer's sultry day;
Through woods and floods he pass'd, and o'er the boist'rous main,
Nor e'er was known to shrink, or of his toil complain. . . .

He often rode, as through the land he pass'd,
Full thirty miles before he broke his fast;
Then added thirty more before he stopp'd to dine;
And ten or twenty more before his preaching time.

When worn with toil, and age, and long disease,
He rode an easier way, his friends to please;
But neither friends nor age his wonted speed could stay,
For now he often went his hundred miles a day. . . .

To live for God, while in this vale of tears,
He rose at four o'clock for three-score years;
Then spent the live-long day in something great and good;
Nor lounged one hour away, nor ever ling'ring stood.

That this is no romance, one instance hear,
And may it rend in twain each sluggard's ear!
His last day's work but one he plann'd, and thought to ride
A HUNDRED MILES AND EIGHT, and preach and write beside.

THE ASTONISHING YOUTH

To feed his flock he put forth all his might,
And preach'd the word both morning, noon, and night;
Nor did he ever cease, while we had time to hear,
But preach'd, or someways taught, A THOUSAND TIMES A YEAR.

Besides the rest, which we assert as facts,
He wrote in all about two hundred tracts;
And yet, in every year, a thousand missives sent
Through this and various isles, and every continent. . . .

At last the mortal foe his dart prepared;
We saw and wept, and each his grief declared;
Then tried each fruitless means to shield his sacred head;
Nor would we cease to try when all our hopes were fled. . . .

But he, unmoved, beheld his end draw nigh,
And met the coming foe without a sigh;
Then raised his feeble voice, though with a falt'ring tongue,
And spread his arms abroad, and thus divinely sung. . . .

As Isr'el mourn'd of old, his fav'rite gone:
And Rachel mourn'd her fertile plains along;
As Mary mourn'd and wept beneath her Saviour's cross;
So we, with moans and tears, will now lament our loss.

For this let us, like him, the world disdain;
For this, like him, rejoice in toil and pain;
Like him, be bold for God; like him, our time redeem;
And strive, and watch, and pray; and live and die like him.

THE TESTIMONY OF HIS FAMILY AND FRIENDS

Finally, John Pawson, one of the most famous of Wesley's preachers, may be chosen to describe the effect of John Wesley's serious illness of 1783 upon all his 'sons in the Gospel'.[26] He said that at the Conference in Bristol the minds of the preachers were 'deeply affected' and that many fervent prayers were offered up on Wesley's behalf. He further stated that Wesley was 'meek, patient, resigned, and as a little child'. In 1791 however he sadly recorded that 'the Lord called home our spiritual Joshua'.

There is much evidence that this was the true relationship. None was more solicitous of the well-being of his helpers. He knew them by their Christian names. He advised on their love affairs with as much interest as on their reading. He gave them extra financial help in time of extra need. He listened to their complaints and the difficulties of their work, and he advised them on the spiritual welfare of their societies. Always he was ready to applaud them and always ready to encourage.

Nevertheless, though they loved him as one who shared their hardships, knew their circumstances, and called them 'brothers' because he meant it, they did realize that his power was such that it could only be possessed by himself, and that when he died it must be shared by all. There is a revealing letter from

[26] *The Lives of Early Methodist Preachers,* IV.58.

Christopher Hopper, one of Wesley's early assistants, to Joseph Cownley.[27] Referring to John Wesley he says: 'I think the old man must reign his day and how we are to be governed after I cannot tell. I leave it to One who cannot err. . . . I hope his latter end will be peace and glory.' It was the same Hopper who said to Joseph Benson, a scholarly and able preacher in the Society, who had raised the query of publishing his sermons: 'If you should make haste to publish them, your sermons may not meet with that approbation among Methodists which you expect. You know how we are circumstanced. If Mr Wesley only speaks a word against them or gives a frown, that is enough. Thousands will neither buy, see, nor read them.'[28]

Thus the preachers were not unaware of his weaknesses. Joseph Benson spoke for many when he said in a letter to Wesley (1769) that he could not endure contradiction and that he favoured those who flattered. In his reply (3rd December 1769) John Wesley refuted the charges as being written 'in a spirit of discontent'. Plainly, however, there was just sufficient truth to make him wince.

Yet the mood of the preachers to the end was one of affection, mixed with a certain quiet determination to have no second Pope. Perhaps it was for that reason that Dr Coke was passed over and the early presidents

---

[27] Dated Colne, 6th April 1780; cf. *Journal*, VI.270, note.
[28] See my *John Wesley and the Eighteenth Century*, p. 18.

chosen after 1791 were excellent men but not ambitious or powerful. The true sentiment of the preachers toward Wesley was expressed in the sense of overwhelming loss and loneliness when death took him from their midst.

WHY HE WAS LOVED

CHAPTER THREE

WHY HE WAS LOVED

THE CONCLUSION which follows from his hold over the affections of so wide a circle is that John Wesley was not only respected for his work but liked for himself.

What were the reasons for the universal esteem in which he was held? The man who would have friends must be friendly; he who would be loved must be capable of loving. John Wesley was a great lover of his fellows. One of our conventional modes of greeting is to ask, 'How are you?' but no detailed reply is expected, and if we receive one we look upon the person who gives it as a bore, for the classic definition of a bore is one who talks of himself when you want to talk of yourself. John Wesley, however, genuinely wanted to know people's state of health, and some of his correspondence with his friends was occupied with suggestions of remedies for their ailments. A week before his brother Charles died, when John was seriously troubled over his illness, he wrote a letter to his niece Sally which, apart from the last paragraph, consisted wholly of prescriptions. These included binding either a split onion or thin slices of beef to the stomach and drinking a medicine

THE ASTONISHING YOUTH

compounded of boiled white bread, lemon juice, and a little loaf sugar.[1]

As early as 1748 John Wesley had divided London into twenty-three parts with two visitors for the sick of each division. He declared that for six-and-twenty years anatomy and physic had been the diversion of his leisure hours, and so he proferred advice to those who needed it. 'In five months', he said, 'medicines were given occasionally to above five hundred persons.'[2] In 1749 he issued his *Primitive Physick*, which despite the seeming quaintness of many recipes was well abreast of existing medical opinion and which passed through thirty editions.[3] Thus from beginning to end of his ministry John Wesley was genuinely interested in people's bodily health.

But this was only because he was interested in people themselves. Among his letters there is one to Samuel Bardsley (5th August 1771) in which he says he had intended to send him to a more distant circuit, but 'we can hardly show enough tenderness for an aged parent. Therefore for your mother's sake I will alter my design and appoint you for the Derbyshire Circuit.' The *Journal*, too, bears record of his ceaseless interest in his fellows. There is no more exciting story in the early annals of Methodism than that of

[1] 20th March 1788.
[2] *A Plain Account of the People called Methodists* (1748), *Works*, VIII.263-4. See also Letter to Mr John Smith, 25th June 1746, ibid. XII.88-9.
[3] See *John Wesley Among the Physicians*, A. Wesley Hill (Epworth Press, 1958).

WHY HE WAS LOVED

Martha Thompson, who came from Preston to London to enter domestic service. She heard John Wesley preach on Moorfields, was converted, and henceforth was continually singing at her work. Because her mistress believed her to be mad she spirited her away to Bedlam. Shut up in a lunatic asylum far from any friends who cared for her, Martha still found courage to sing,

> *I love His name, I love His word,*
> *Join all my powers to praise the Lord.*

After many months of confinement she was able through a gentleman visitor to the Asylum to get a letter to John Wesley. He read the account of her sufferings and immediately sent two doctors to investigate her case. They reported that she was sane and fit to be discharged. Wesley thereupon asked her to meet him at the Foundery. When he heard her story and discovered that she wanted to return to Preston he took her with him on his next journey to the North of England. Mounted behind him on his horse she travelled with him as far as Stafford. He then booked a seat for her in a coach that was going to Manchester and gave her sufficient money to get home. Then, because he had already gone out of his way, he turned back his horse's head to fulfil engagements in Wolverhampton and the Black Country. Martha Thompson founded Methodism in Preston and welcomed John Wesley on each of his four visits.

THE ASTONISHING YOUTH

Not always did his concern for people bear such astonishing fruit.

The *Journal* abounds in records of the scores of people he met and conversed with in his journeyings. Among them was the man who 'very calmly and deliberately' had beaten his wife with a large stick till she was black and blue from head to foot. He insisted it was his duty because she was so surly and ill-natured, and he assured Wesley that 'he was full of faith all the time he was doing it'.[4]

Wesley's liking for people was extended to children. Having no children of his own he was father to all the children in the Methodist societies. He recorded that after he had preached in Bolton an army of children got around him and he could scarcely disengage himself from them.[5] On another occasion he persuaded 'a host of children' to come into the house where he was staying and to sing: 'Vital spark of heavenly flame'. He declared that the harmony could not be equalled in the King's Chapel.[6] On another occasion Wesley filled his coach with children and for the space of an hour took them a ride round the town.

Mathias Joyce, a Roman Catholic, went to hear John Wesley preach in Dublin. He said afterwards that what impressed him most was to see John Wesley stoop down and kiss a little child that sat upon the

[4] IV.204. [5] *Journal*, VII.155, 16th April 1786.
[6] Ibid. VII.306, 27th July 1787.

pulpit stairs.[7] Southey himself told of the way he felt drawn to Wesley when he saw the old man kiss his little sister.

Add to Wesley's humanity his boundless interest in life, and one can further understand his hold over people. He freely gave his opinion on such divers and unusual subjects as air balloons, the effect of music on animals, the moon, foxgloves, glass, laburnum, lions, paintings, and ventriloquists. He would go out of his way to see an unusual building or some gentleman's gardens and park. He observed the changing face of England and recorded the growth of the industrial North. Through his eyes one can almost follow the rapid rise of Manchester, Leeds, and Liverpool. He was keenly interested in scientific developments, and when he read Benjamin Franklin's *Treatise on Electricity* he knew its importance at once and commented in his *Journal:* 'What an amazing scene is here opened for after-ages to improve upon!'[8] Some years later he published a 72-page pamphlet on the subject.[9] Meanwhile, inspired by Franklin's work, he arranged the construction of an electrical apparatus for the cure of rheumatic disorders. Later he was able to record in his *Journal* (9th November 1756) that many hundreds, perhaps thousands, had received unspeakable good. It is in his *Compendium of Natural Philosophy* that Wesley's scientific curiosity

[7] Mathias Joyce in *The Lives of Early Methodist Preachers*, IV.238.
[8] 17th February 1753.
[9] *The Desideratum or Electricity Made Plain and Useful* (1760).

is best revealed. He wrote 'Of Man', 'Of Brutes', 'Of Plants', and 'Of Natural Bodies'. His statement of the *scala naturae* owed much to Bonnet and to Buffon, and was one of the early foreshadowings of the discoveries of Darwin.[10] Nothing human seemed alien to Wesley and nothing seemed to be a bore.

In all this preoccupation with the human scene Wesley allowed neither jealousy nor rancour nor resentment to cloud his relations with others. Whether he was dealing with Selina Countess of Huntingdon, or an Anglican bishop, or one of his own preachers, his tone was always the same. He could not be arrogant nor could he be obsequious. In whatever company, he remained natural and unaffected, judging a man in himself and never by his station in life. How could it be otherwise? He declared that he loved the poor and found in many of them pure genuine grace unmixed with folly and affectation; on the other hand, after he had spent two or three hours in the House of Lords, he declared; 'I had frequently heard that this was the most venerable assembly in England. But how was I disappointed! What is a Lord but a sinner born to die.'[11]

Closely allied with this detachment of mind was Wesley's remarkable self-control. The irascible Charles was the son of the short-tempered Rector of Epworth, but John had his mother's patience and

[10] *A Survey of the Wisdom of God in the Creation* or *A Compendium of Philosophy*, 5 vols (4th edn, 1784).
[11] *Journal*, VII.46, 25th January 1785.

WHY HE WAS LOVED

calmness of mind. Even when he was most provoked he showed no anger. When Charles behaved so outrageously in the case of Grace Murray, and John lost the woman he loved, he only noted; 'My brother's impetuosity prevailed and bore down all before it.' When the two brothers met in the presence of George Whitefield and John Nelson they embraced each other and wept. John Wesley heard Grace Murray's assurance that she had said no word against him, and his successful rival John Bennet's plea for pardon in any ill word he had spoken. 'Between them both', said John, 'I knew not what to say or do. I can forgive. But who can redress the wrong?' Three years later (29th October 1752) he commented justly in his *Journal:* 'If I have any strength at all, and I have none but what I have received, it is in forgiving injuries.'

All his self-control and magnanimity were needed when, still under the smarting loss of Grace he had been nursed in sickness by Mrs Vazeille, a predatory widow, and had married that 'woman of sorrowful spirit'. She had the hard choice of grass widowhood for many months of each year or the arduous life of accompanying him on his missionary journeys. She tried both and found them equally repugnant. There remained only her waspish tongue and venomous pen to make him miserable, since she could not change his course of life. In the long story of her endless recriminations, that 'extreme immeasurable bitterness' of which John spoke, one incident will always stand

THE ASTONISHING YOUTH

out more clearly than the rest. It would appear that Mrs Wesley had stolen some of her husband's letters and had mutilated them with a view to publication. Charles was horrified and urged his brother to return to Bristol and stop the slanders. John Wesley's reply was unforgettable: 'Brother, when I devoted to God my ease, my time, my life, did I except my reputation? No. Tell Sally[12] I will take her to Canterbury tomorrow.'

Until the last ten years of his life, when John Wesley had outlived all calumny, he was subject at all times to irate men abusing his person and traducing his work. In all this sea of hot-tempered misrepresentation there is not one instance of Wesley losing his temper or replying in kind to his accusers. The hotter they became, the cooler he was. Perhaps the reason for this astonishing freedom from anger may be found in chance remarks. He said in a letter to Ebenezer Blackwell (31st August 1755) that he was content with whatever entertainment he met with and that his companions were always in a good temper because they were with him. He wanted that to be the spirit of all who journeyed with him. 'If a dinner ill-dressed, or a hard bed, a poor room, a shower of rain or a dusty road will put them out of humour, it lays a burthen on me greater than all the rest put together.' Then follow words which are deservedly famous as offering

[12] Sally was Charles's daughter and John Wesley's niece. *Journal*, VI.89, note. Tyerman's account may have been exaggerated, but the substance was true.

an insight to his temperament: 'By the grace of God I never fret, I repine at nothing, I am discontented with nothing. And to hear persons at my ear fretting and murmuring at everything is like tearing flesh off my bones. I see God sitting upon His Throne and ruling all things well.'[13]

When he was preaching in Scotland (16th May 1784) he set at utter defiance the saying, 'He is a good man though he has bad tempers', by declaring: 'Nay, if he has bad tempers, he is no more a good man than the devil is a good angel.' When he was preaching at City Road on the anniversary of the Gunpowder Plot, 5th November 1780, he said: 'The work of God does not, cannot need the work of the devil to forward it. A calm, even spirit goes through rough work far better than a furious one.'

This was all in consonance with his idea of Christian Perfection as 'the humble, gentle, patient love of God and our neighbour, ruling our tempers, words, and actions'.

Analysing charm is always a hazardous undertaking, but another main element in Wesley's appeal to men must have been the vein of dry humour which went with his hatred of pomposity and pretence. Robert Southey blamed Wesley for prohibiting so many innocent diversions for his people, forgetting that he himself needed none because 'wherever he went his presence excited a stir among strangers, and

[13] *Letters*, III.138-9.

made a festival among his friends. Daily change of scene and society . . . kept him in hilarity as well as health.'[14] This trait in Wesley appealed to his famous biographer. He referred elsewhere to his 'playfulness' and the 'cheerful' obedience he obtained from his followers.[15]

Everyone remembers the anecdote so beloved of Augustine Birrell. Wesley in one of his rides fell in with a 'serious' man who wanted to know whether Wesley held the doctrine of the decrees as he himself did. The answers did not please him and at last, so Wesley records, he said; 'I was rotten at heart and supposed I was one of John Wesley's followers. I told him, No, I am John Wesley himself. Upon which he would gladly have run away outright, but being the better mounted of the two, I kept close at his side, and endeavoured to show him his heart until we came into the streets of Northampton!'[16] What gave Birrell his longest chuckle was Wesley's casual use of the revealing phrase 'better mounted' and the thought of the unhappy Calvinist not being able to shake off the Arminian Wesley.

There is no better illustration of his dry wit than the preface he wrote to his *Complete English Dictionary* (1753). 'In compliance with the taste of the age', he said, 'I add that this little Dictionary is not only the shortest and cheapest but likewise by many degrees

[14] *Life of Wesley* (1903 edn), p. 319.   [15] Ibid. p. 222.
[16] *Journal*, III.10, 20th May 1742.

the most correct, which is extant at this day. Many are the mistakes in all the other English Dictionaries which I have yet seen. Whereas I can truly say, I know none in this and I conceive the reader will believe me; for if I had, I should not have left it there.'[17] In that same vein he wrote to Mr Hawes, 'Apothecary and Critic', who had attacked his book of medical remedies: 'Dear Sir, My bookseller informs me that since you published your remarks on the *Primitive Physick* . . . there has been a greater demand for it than ever. If, therefore, you would please to publish a few further remarks, you would confer a further favour on your humble servant.'

Alexander Knox spoke of his 'sportive sallies of innocent mirth', and illustrations abound. On one occasion he said he had spent 'an agreeable hour with Dr S. the greatest genius in little things that ever fell under my notice. I really believe were he seriously to set about it he could invent the best mouse trap that ever was in the world.' 'Stop that man from speaking,' exclaimed Charles Wesley at one of the early Conferences, 'let us attend to business!' Still the good man went on. 'Unless he stops, I'll leave the conference,' said Charles. To which John replied quietly; 'Reach him his hat.' Once when two women were quarrelling violently Sammy Bardsley clutched his arm and said: 'Pray sir, let us go; I cannot stand it.' 'Stay Sammy', said Wesley, 'stay and learn how to preach!'

[17] *Works,* XIV.233-4.

One of Wesley's helpers, Michael Fenwick, came to him whilst he was revising his journals for the Press and asked that his name might be included. John Wesley promised to oblige him and in due course his name appeared: 'About one, preached at Clayworth. I think no one was unmoved save Michael Fenwick, who fell fast asleep under an adjoining hay rick.'[18]

In a letter to Christopher Hopper (7th October 1773) he writes of a portly preacher: 'Peter Jaco would willingly travel. But how? Can you help us to a horse that will carry him and his wife? What a pity we could not procure a camel or an elephant!'

Finally, could any comment be more fitting than Wesley's ironic 'We are forbid to go to Newgate, for fear of making them wicked; and to Bedlam, for fear of driving them mad!'[19]

A man may be liked for his personal charm, but to compel respect bordering upon reverence he must have striking moral qualities. Wesley was entire in his dedication of life. Nothing was held back from God. In his *Rules for the People Called Methodists* and in many pamphlets he eschewed both extravagance in dress and in manner of life; the utmost simplicity was to distinguish the Methodist in his appearance and his conduct. It was advice which he himself practised wholeheartedly. He had found at Oxford he could

[18] *Lectures*, Morley Punshon (1882), p. 330.
[19] *Journal*, III.455, 22nd February 1750.

live on £28 a year, and throughout his life he strove to keep to that minimum standard of requirement. He wore no wig as fashion dictated, had no personal adornments, lived upon a spartan diet, and when asked by the Commissioner of Excise to give an inventory of his valuables, reported that he had two silver spoons at London and two at Bristol. 'This', he said, 'is all the plate which I have at present; and I shall not buy any more, while so many round me want bread.'[20]

A horsehair shirt, however, has never yet endeared a saint to a sinner. His austerities would not have commended him had he not worn the rough shirt as though it had been silk. Wesley ignored much that others considered the necessities of life. He had a chosen work to do and he was not to be deflected from it. This inflexibility of purpose was partly derived from his ancestry. Were not both his paternal and his maternal grandfathers ejected from their livings on the ill-fated St Bartholomew's Day 1662? Refusal to accept the Act of Uniformity led the former, the Rev. John Wesley, after persecution and imprisonment to an early death. The latter, Dr Samuel Annesley, was more fortunate, because his scholarship and preaching made him the natural leader of dissenters in London; but both men forsook ease and comfort when they left the shelter of their vicarages for a totally new and uncertain prospect.[21]

[20] *Journal*, VI.26, note.   [21] See *Family Circle*, pp. 1, 2, 6.

THE ASTONISHING YOUTH

John Wesley's parents did not allow the recollection of such great sacrifice to determine their own thinking. Independently of each other they became dissatisfied with Dissent and by conviction returned to the Anglican fold. The point therefore is not that he had dissenting blood in his veins, but that all his forebears showed qualities of resolution and initiative, and these he amply inherited. Even his initial break with accepted custom required courage. There had been no open-air preaching in England since the days of the Lollards, and everyone knew what had happened to them. He did more than overcome his own fastidiousness and sense of the proprieties when on 2nd April 1739 he 'submitted to be more vile' and preached in Bristol to three thousand people.[22] He was not only courting the resentment of clergy and gentry but ignoring his own regard for Anglican etiquette when he overstepped parish boundaries. In all his subsequent 'irregular' actions of appointing laymen as his assistants, founding Methodist Societies, licensing his chapels,[23] ordaining men for the work overseas, and fashioning his Deed of Declaration,[24] he might well have said: 'I can do no other, so help me God.' They were all actions by which he separated himself from the Church of his first love, but he was driven on by a sense of inner moral

[22] *Journal*, II.172-3, and footnotes.
[23] Ibid. VII.339, 3rd November 1787.
[24] Ibid. VI.481, 28th March 1784. The 'legal hundred' ministers of the Conference became his heirs.

compulsion. It was not only his ancestral blood which enabled him to endure persecution and obloquy for his convictions; it was the consciousness that only so could God's work be accomplished by him.

To this tenacity of purpose were allied remarkable powers of leadership. When he left home for Charterhouse, one might have supposed that a school which was known at that period for the severity of its discipline, and in which—as contemporary accounts agree —there was a system of brutal flogging, would break his heart. On the contrary he always spoke well of his old school, and its Spartan way of life dismayed him not at all. In later life he revisited the school,[25] and as a good Carthusian spoke of his joy in meeting old friends and reflecting on the 'dream of the fifty or sixty years' since they were together at school'.[26] John Wesley had already taken his degree at Christ Church and had served as his father's curate at Wroote before he returned to take up his fellowship at Lincoln College. The Holy Club had meanwhile been started by his brother Charles, but John at once assumed the leadership when he joined the little group. One of its first members, Robert Kirkham, expressed in a letter his admiration for the Oxford Scholar: 'Your most deserving character, your worthy personal accomplishments, your noble endowments of mind, your little and handsome person, and your obliging and

[25] See especially *Journal*, II.77, 129d, 131d, 132, X.232.
[26] Ibid. V.276.

desirable conversation, have been the pleasing subject of our discourse for some pleasant hours.' The ageing Rector of Epworth was so pleased with their devotional life and their works of charity that he wrote to say he blessed God for two sons in Oxford 'to whom He has given grace and courage to turn even against the world and the devil'. 'Go on', he said, 'in the path to which your Saviour has directed you, and the track wherein your father has gone before you.'[27]

Although John resisted his father's pressing invitation to follow him as Rector of Epworth,[28] he was ready seven months later to sail for Georgia. He went, as he said in a letter to Dr John Burton (10th October 1735), to save his own soul and to do more good in America than would be possible at home. When he arrived he found both these objectives most difficult of accomplishment. General Oglethorpe, impressed by John Wesley's outstanding ability and the immense service he could render to the colony, favoured his growing friendship with Sophy Hopkey, trusting that it would result in marriage. Thomas Causton, the chief magistrate of Savannah and Sophia's uncle, also strongly desired the marriage because it would strengthen his own social standing. Wesley, by birth, education, and leadership, was already the major force for good within the colony, but he was ever the awkward and difficult suitor. At a time when ardour

[27] 28th September 1730.   [28] 10th December 1734.

would have moved the more impetuous to a proposal, Wesley could write somewhat chillingly; 'I find, Miss Sophy, I can't take fire into my bosom and not be burnt. I am therefore retiring for a while to desire the direction of God. Join me, my friend, in fervent prayer that he would show me what is best to be done.' Small wonder that the lovely and youthful Sophy was piqued by so hesitant a lover, and accepted William Williamson who was restrained by no such misgivings.

Sophy's marriage and John's ill-advised refusal on ecclesiastical grounds to admit her to Communion incensed her family, divided the colony, and made his position in Georgia untenable. But it is not just to regard his stay in Georgia as a failure. Throughout its course he was the devoted priest, living according to strict method and serving the mental and spiritual needs of his flock. After his prayers, reading and writing in the morning, he used the afternoon for visiting the sick and for teaching pupils Greek, Hebrew, French, German, Church History, Canon Law, and—in the case of John Reinier—anatomy.[29] Three times a day he read the prayers and twice a day he expounded the Scriptures. Although this routine was broken by journeyings on land and sea, visits to Oglethorpe, and occasional bouts of sickness, he always resumed his orderly ministry with the utmost despatch.

[29] See *Journal*, I, 'The Georgian Journal', 14th October 1735–1st February 1738.

THE ASTONISHING YOUTH

It was during this period that some characteristic institutions of later Methodism were started, such as the society class and the select bands.[30] Most important of all was the publication of the *Collection of Hymns and Psalms* in Charleston in 1737. This is memorable not only as the first hymn-book of the Wesleys, but because in it are included some of John Wesley's magnificent translations of hymns from the German.

Wesley suffered in Georgia from his unworldliness, his unyielding Caroline brand of Churchmanship, and his lack of judgement in dealing with others. Yet none can deny his authority in the colony and the strange compound of respect and fear he aroused even in those who were his foes.

In England Peter Böhler, the Moravian, was under God the chief instrument in his conversion. As early as 18th February 1738 he warned Wesley that his philosophy must be purged away. On 4th March he gave further significant advice. Wesley had wondered whether he ought to leave off preaching because he had not saving faith himself, and he received counsel: 'Preach faith till you have it, and then because you have it, you will preach faith.' Finally Peter Böhler brought Wesley to know that a man can be saved in an instant of time. He brought forward several witnesses 'who testified God had thus wrought in themselves, giving them in a moment such a faith in the blood of his Son as translated them out of darkness

[30] Cf. *Journal*, I.197-8 (April 1736) and notes.

into light'. Wesley said: 'Here ended my disputing. I could now only cry out Lord, help thou my unbelief.'[31]

On 4th May Peter Böhler embarked for Carolina, and much later Wesley added in his *Journal* for this date: 'O what a work hath God begun, since his coming to England! Such a one as shall never come to an end till heaven and earth pass away.'

Böhler's last service was to write him a letter in which he pleaded with him not to delay but 'to believe in your Jesus Christ'. Even Böhler, however, could hardly have believed the delay would be so short. On 24th May the day began with intolerable heaviness of spirit and ended with a strange warmness of heart. In the afternoon at St Paul's the anthem 'Out of the deep I have cried unto thee O Lord' matched his sombre mood but could not relieve it. Very unwillingly he went to a little meeting-house in Aldersgate Street and the miracle happened. Because of a swift understanding of what Luther meant in his *Preface to the Romans* he felt he did trust in Christ, Christ alone for salvation, and an assurance was given him that Christ had taken away *his* sins, even *his*, and delivered *him* from the law of sin and death. The time was a quarter to nine and no hour has been more significant for the modern world.

Wesley had been a leader in Georgia, but he lacked followers. This was partly because he had gone to

[31] Ibid. p. 455, 23rd April 1738.

save his own soul and was overmuch occupied with his own struggles. He described himself in Savannah as 'fighting continually, but not conquering' and as striving with, but not freed from sin.[32]

A man can never fight effectively for God when he is fighting within himself. Wesley's natural powers of leadership could only be fully employed when he was released from this introspective and inhibiting struggle. The whole difference between Wesley before and after conversion lies in the fact that before 24th May 1738 he was continually asking what he could do; afterwards he only asked what God could do for him. In modern terms it would be explained as a difference in his psychological attitude to life. The great mystics who influenced him in Oxford days were Thomas à Kempis, Jeremy Taylor, William Law, and Henry Scougal. All of them, to use the title of Scougal's great book, spoke of 'the life of God in the soul of man', and under their guidance John Wesley gave himself up to the cultivation of the interior life. By prayer, fasting, and meditation, by study of the Bible, by attendance at God's house and by waiting upon the Lord's Table, he had sought vainly to achieve a reconciliation with God. Like an intrepid climber he sought to scale the mount of heaven.

He was saved from an unhealthy mysticism, not only because he used the appointed means of grace,

[32] *Journal*, I.470.

WHY HE WAS LOVED

but because his strongly practical bent of mind sent him out of an Oxford College into the Oxford jail, the Oxford poor-house, and the hovels of the sick and needy. Georgia was but a further essay in his quest for God.

Father Maximin Piette points out quite rightly that since 1725 his life had been that of a regulated Christian. Even Wesley himself on one occasion wrote to brother Charles, '*Vitae me redde priori!*[33] let me be again an Oxford Methodist. I am often in doubt whether it would not be best for me to resume all my Oxford rules, great and small. I did then walk closely with God and redeem the time. But what have I been doing these thirty years.'[34]

But on that occasion, looking back romantically over the years, he was forgetting his former state of mind. Despite the exceptional quality of his Christian living he did not know peace of mind nor release of spirit. Consequently he had neither a sense of acceptance with God, nor a sense of power. Upon his conversion, however, he had deliverance and assurance and strength. He expressed it in his own words as he ruminated on his conversion experience: 'Herein I found where the difference between this and my former state chiefly consisted. I was striving, yea, fighting, with all my might under the law, as well as under grace. But then I was sometimes, if not

---
[33] 'Give me back my former life'—a quotation from Horace.
[34] 15th December 1772.

often, conquered: now I was always conqueror.'[35]

For the rest of his life he was to fret at nothing nor repine. He was to sleep soundly at night undisturbed by man's power to hurt the body or the mind. He was to remain calm whilst incensed opponents were raging against him. He was to be jealous of God's honour but entirely careless of his own reputation. He was to be entirely composed even when his brother was tense. In a word, he was not to undertake for God but allow God to undertake for him. This 'recumbency on God', this recruiting of strength from God, gave him the power and the peace and the joy which in former days were lacking. It heightened all his natural powers, so that he was *facile princeps* in whatever company he moved. A natural leader had become by supernatural grace a maker of history and a prince of the Church.

[35] *Journal*, I.477, 24th May 1738. Compare that early Wesley hymn which surely may have been written by John since it is a poetic transcription of his experience:

> *I wrestle not now, but trample on sin,*
> *For with me art thou, and shalt be within;*
> *While stronger and stronger in Jesus's power,*
> *I go on to conquer, till sin is no more.*

THE DECADES OF HIS MINISTRY

CHAPTER FOUR

THE DECADES OF HIS MINISTRY

IN EACH remaining decade of his life this remarkable effortless mastery over men may be illustrated. The first ten years of the Revival were marked by conflict and controversy. Stirred up by squire and parson the mobs were often in ugly mood, and the Methodist people were not without their martyrs. In these circumstances it is the more astonishing that John and his brother Charles escaped with only minor hurt when their lives were constantly in danger.

John Wesley was born before the days of psychology, but he knew by intuition that you stare your enemy in the face; you never show him your back. In the notorious Wednesbury riots of February 1744[1] the ringleader was an 'honest' Joe Munchin, whose great bulk and savage bearing might have intimidated the bravest. John Wesley forced his way to him and asked what he wanted. 'Honest Joe', who a minute before would have cheerfully clubbed him, now in stupefaction brought his hand gently down and remarked on the silkiness of his hair. Through Munchin's self-imposed protection Wesley was kept from further harm, and when one day the ringleader was

[1] See *Journal*, III.116-19. Also *Modern Christianity Exemplified at Wednesbury* (2nd edn, 1745).

THE ASTONISHING YOUTH

converted, the adjective describing him was truly earned.

At Falmouth[2] the following year Wesley found a house he had visited beset 'by an innumerable multitude' of people. He compared the storm they made to the raging of the sea. His friends besought him to hide, but he said: 'No, it is best for me to stand just where I am.' By sheer pressure the mob tore the door from its hinges, and at once John Wesley stepped forward bareheaded, for he purposely wanted them to see his face. 'Here I am', he said. 'Which of you has anything to say to me? To which have I done any harm?' Taking advantage of their astonishment he asked if he might speak, and proceeded steadily to address them even though only a handful could hear. Wesley in retrospect was himself amazed, because 'although the hands of perhaps some hundreds were lifted up to strike or throw, yet they were one and all stopped in midway so that not one man touched me with one of his fingers'.[3] Two or three gentlemen, including a Rev. Mr Thomas, brought him away totally unharmed.

Coming to Plymouth on 27th June 1747 he found himself besieged by a great multitude. Seeing 'the violence of the rabble increasing' he walked into the thickest part and 'took the captain of the mob by the hand'; the man was so surprised that he said: 'Sir, I will see you safe home. No man shall touch you. . . .

[2] *Journal*, III.188-9, 4th July 1745. [3] Ibid. p. 190.

I will knock the first man down that touches you.' Wesley adds with a touch of quiet humour: 'We then parted in much love.'[4]

The period of rioting came to a close in the last year of the decade,[5] but the Cork riots were certainly as terrible as any in England. On 20th May he came out of the house where he had preached to find a mob on all sides hemming him in. He describes what happened. 'I walked straight on through the midst of the rabble looking every man before me in the face, and they opened right and left till I came near Daunt's Bridge. A large party had taken possession of this, one of whom was barking out, "Now, hey for the Romans!" I came up and they likewise shrank back and I walked through them to Mr Jenkins's house.'[6]

In all these instances John Wesley not only showed high personal courage but confounded his would-be persecutors by advancing to the leader with entire fearlessness and demanding to know what had he done. There was a rare quality of leadership shining from his face and showing itself in his bearing which made his detractors fall shamedly away from him. He was the master of circumstances because he was a master of men.

The decade of the fifties was dominated by the Seven Years War. When war with France broke out in 1756 John Wesley was so much in control of his

[4] Ibid. p. 304.   [5] May 1750.   [6] *Journal*, III.471.

Societies that he could write with entire confidence to the Hon. James West[7] offering to raise a company of two hundred volunteers for His Majesty's service to be supported by contributions among themselves and to be ready in case of an invasion to act for a year at His Majesty's pleasure. He concluded by asking for them to have arms on the usual security for their return and some of His Majesty's sergeants to instruct them.

Three years later he heard that French prisoners of war were being quartered at Knowle near Bristol. When he investigated for himself he found that eleven hundred were 'confined in a little place without anything to lie on but a little dirty straw or anything to cover them but a few foul thin rags'. They died, he said, 'like rotten sheep'. He was horrified, and that night preached in Bristol from the text: 'Thou shalt not oppress a stranger: for ye know the heart of a stranger, seeing ye were strangers in the land of Egypt.'[8] He made a collection with which to supply them with clothing, stirred up the Corporation of Bristol to send mattresses and blankets, wrote a powerful letter to *Lloyd's Evening Post* which brought many contributions from London, and was at last satisfied that the prisoners were 'pretty well provided with all the necessaries of life.' Alas! The next year he found them 'almost naked again' and he wrote in the *Journal*: 'In the hopes of provoking others to

[7] 1st March 1756.   [8] Exodus 23⁹.

THE DECADES OF HIS MINISTRY

jealousy I made another collection for them and ordered the money to be laid out in linen and waistcoats which were given to those most in want.'[9] The whole incident is a striking example of Wesley's quick appraisal of a situation, his willingness to act immediately, and his initiative in stirring others to similar activity.

As the editor of the Standard Edition of the *Journal* was quick to note, the man who figured most prominently in the third decade of Wesley's itinerancy was Thomas Maxfield.

John Cennick may claim credit for being the first lay preacher but Maxfield was the true pioneer of lay preaching in the Methodist Church. It will not be forgotten that when Susanna Wesley came to live at the Foundery in the last three years of her life, Thomas Maxfield was a young man who in John Wesley's absence was fully capable not only of reading the Scriptures in gatherings of the Society but of offering his own extended interpretation. When John Wesley heard what was happening he rode back to London in great perturbation of spirit. He was met by his mother who cautioned him to take care what he did. Wesley heard Maxfield for himself and then acknowledged that it was God's ordering.

Maxfield, following Cennick, became the first of an army of lay preachers who made possible the

[9] IV.417, 24th October 1760.

THE ASTONISHING YOUTH

spread of Methodism throughout the country, and helped to supply the meeting-houses with preachers as they were built. He must have been a man of charm as well as parts. He was not only respected and admired by such leaders as Lady Huntingdon, but by John Wesley himself. It was during this third decade that a woman said to Wesley: 'Sir, I employ several men. Now, if one of my servants will not follow my direction is it not right for me to discard him at once? Pray do you apply this to Mr Bell. He answered: 'It is right to discard such a servant; but what would you do if he were your son?' Bell could be dismissed as a crankish visionary, but Maxfield was different. He was a 'son in the gospel'.[10]

This makes all the more remarkable Wesley's strong and effective handling of him. Here a strong personal liking was in conflict with an equally strong sense of discipline. Consistent with the unity and peace of the Society, John Wesley did all he could to keep Maxfield. At his insistence the Bishop of Derry ordained him priest, 'To assist that good man that he may not work himself to death'.[11] Maxfield neither accepted a benefice nor stayed within Methodism. Wesley set down in detail the steps which led up to separation and the exemplary patience he had shown.[12] Despite objections from many preachers and Methodist people, John Wesley 'continually and strenuously

[10] 1st January 1763.   [11] *Journal*, V.11.   [12] Ibid. V.10-13.

defended him', but this did not prevent Maxfield from complaining that he had never been so persecuted by the rabble in Cornwall as he had by the brothers Wesley.

He encouraged several fanatics who claimed to have dreams and visions from God to come under his ministry. They said: 'Blind John (i.e. John Wesley) is not capable of teaching us; we will keep to Mr Maxfield.' But the final point of departure was reached when John Wesley told his preachers they could not in conscience preach at Snowsfields, since the layman in charge was allowing the misguided, deluded George Bell to preach there. When Maxfield refused to comply, Wesley sent him a note asking him to desist, adding: 'If you do [preach at Snowsfields], you thereby renounce connexion with me.' At once Maxfield rejoined, 'I *will* preach at Snowsfields', and the knot was cut. Wesley wrote in his *Journal*: 'So the breach is made; but I am clear, I have done all I possibly could to prevent it. I walked immediately away, and preached on "If I am bereaved of my children, I am bereaved".'[13]

There can be no doubt of Wesley's wisdom in letting Maxfield go. The underlying weakness of the man was his impatience of authority. He learnt neither self-discipline nor obedience. His sympathetic association with the weak-minded Bell and his advocacy of a Christian Perfection which expressed itself in

[13] Ibid. V.10, 28th March 1763.

emotional excesses made it imperative that he should go.

But the final parting and the manifest ingratitude of Maxfield cut John Wesley to the quick. He described himself as 'His father, his friend, his greatest earthly benefactor', and yet he declared that Maxfield had spoken ill of him 'for six weeks together'. Maxfield, as an independent minister, stayed for a few years at Snowsfields Chapel, then removed to Ropemaker's Alley, and on to Princess Street in Moorfields.[14] In his fury of spirit he wrote in 1767 his *Vindication*, an apologia which John Wesley described as 'That wretched book'. In February 1773 when they met, Thomas Maxfield tried to blame Lady Huntingdon and George Whitefield for persuading him to write the book. His explanation revealed his uneasy mind and Wesley received his words with a certain polite reserve.[15]

In his dealings with Thomas Maxfield Wesley displayed two qualities possessed only by essentially strong characters. He was magnanimous in his personal dealings with the offended, despite the fact that Maxfield had been for fifteen years the source of disaffection in the London Society.[16] This was shown by his willingness to preach twice in Maxfield's church in Moorfields[17] and to visit him when he was gravely ill.[18] Nevertheless, he did not weaken in his condem-

[14] *Journal*, V.7, note. See also Wilson's *History of Dissenting Meeting-Houses*. [15] Ibid. V.498, 4th February 1773.
[16] Cf. *Journal*, VI.180, note. [17] Ibid. p. 389. [18] Ibid. pp. 383, 431.

nation of Maxfield's errors[19] nor seek to keep him when his unreadiness to accept the Methodist discipline was finally manifest.

It was the same leader of men who faced the mobs in the forties, supplied the needs of French prisoners in the fifties, and dealt firmly but kindly with an outstanding but rebellious preacher in the sixties. The same strength of personality was even more dramatically displayed when he was called upon to deal with the Calvinist controversy in the fourth decade of his ministry. There was never any real possibility of the Countess of Huntingdon and John Wesley coming to a lasting agreement, because each ruled in their own right and would not brook another's interference. Lady Huntingdon found George Whitefield much more to her liking, because he was willing amply to acknowledge her superior station, whilst Wesley, with a touch of aristocratic hauteur, treated her with courtesy but no deference; but in any case the Calvinist views of Whitefield were altogether to her liking. Whilst Whitefield lived, however, the bond between Lady Huntingdon and John Wesley and their respective supporters was not broken. When Wesley wrote to her offering to preach in her chapel at Bath she gratefully accepted, and went on: 'I do trust that this union which has commenced will be for the furtherance of our faith and mutual love to each

[19] Cf. his reply to Thomas Maxfield's pamphlet in 1778; *Works*, XI.478.

THE ASTONISHING YOUTH

other. It is for the interest of the best of causes that we should all be found first faithful to the Lord and then to each other. I find something wanting, and that is a meeting now and then agreed upon, that you, your brother, Mr Whitefield and I, should at times regularly be glad to communicate our observations upon the state of the work!'[20] John Wesley preached at the Countess of Huntingdon's chapel on the evening of 25th August 1766 and commented that 'many were not a little surprised'.[21] On Sunday 5th October he was back again, and Horace Walpole, the dilettante man of letters, heard the sermon and wrote to his friend John Chute that Wesley was 'Wondrous clever, but as evidently an actor as Garrick. . . . toward the end, he exalted his voice, and acted very ugly enthusiasm.' Wesley's judgement on the service was very different. He said the word was quick and powerful.[22]

Early in 1769 Charles Wesley prayed and John Wesley preached in Lady Huntingdon's London house in Portland Row, Cavendish Square, and John, who approved the large and attentive congregation but suspected fashionable assemblies, wrote ironically: 'Let us despair of nothing.'[23] In the summer he joined the leaders of the evangelical revival at the celebrations of the first anniversary of Trevecca

---

[20] *The Arminian Magazine* (1796), p. 304, contains the full copy of the letter.
[21] *Journal*, V.183.   [22] Ibid. p. 188.
[23] Ibid. p. 304, 5th March 1769.

THE DECADES OF HIS MINISTRY

College, which had been opened by Lady Huntingdon for the training of preachers on 24th August 1768; Wesley preached in the evening and John Fletcher preached an exceedingly lively sermon the following morning.[24] There can be no doubt that at this time the Countess sincerely desired that her college might be used for both wings of the Revival. Shortly after this gathering she appointed Joseph Benson, a Methodist preacher, as headmaster, and the Rev. John Fletcher was a frequent visitor.

But the halcyon days were not to last. In 1770 George Whitefield died, and although Wesley preached his funeral sermon on 18th November at the Tottenham Court Road Chapel, his death caused the two sections to fall apart. His friendship with Wesley survived all their differences of opinion and in his will it was his oldest friend John Wesley to whom he bequeathed a mourning ring and whom he asked to preach his funeral sermon. Whilst he lived the Calvinist detractors of John Wesley were kept in leash, but when his strong influence was removed they felt free to turn and rend their theological opponents in pieces.

With Lady Huntingdon it was not only the death of Whitefield but her newly formed friendship with the aristocratic family of the Hills which opened a breach with the Methodists. Both Sir Richard and Rowland Hill were pronouncedly Calvinistic in their

[24] Ibid. p. 334.

views, and they served therefore to deepen Lady Huntingdon's bias against an Arminian view of grace. Under their influence she became persuaded that the *Conference Minutes* of 1770 were heretical. At her dictation her cousin the Rev. and Hon. Walter Shirley sent a circular letter to a large number of Calvinist sympathizers summoning them to a meeting in Bristol at a time coincident with Wesley's annual Conference. Students and ministers who did not disown the 1770 *Minutes* were forced to leave, and Joseph Benson was dismissed.

John Fletcher, 'an angry lamb in fight', resented this attack and wrote five letters addressed to Walter Shirley. When the manuscript was put into John Wesley's hands he published it as the *First Check to Antinomianism*. The publication grieved Shirley and the Countess, but it infuriated the younger Calvinists, who declared war to the death. Strangely, the Calvinist *Gospel Magazine*, in all the scurrilous attacks of those years, assailed Wesley himself rather than Fletcher. When the Calvinist Conference met in Bristol, John Wesley was asked to receive a deputation, and on Thursday 6th August Walter Shirley arrived with nine or ten others. With Wesley's consent he read two letters written by Lady Huntingdon and himself, which had been received by Wesley the evening befor the Conference. A two-hour discussion followed, and Wesley tersely commented that 'they were satisfied we were not so dreadful heretics as they

THE DECADES OF HIS MINISTRY

imagined, but were tolerably sound in the faith'. Conflicting accounts of the Conference were given,[25] but it would seem that after the joint signing of a declaration drawn up by Wesley, Shirley acknowledged publicly that he had mistaken the meaning of the *Minutes*. It was in fact a rout of the Calvinist forces, who had stormed the Conference fortress with insufficient ammunition. Shirley retreated in discomfort to give his own version of the sorry affair.

It can well be imagined that Her Ladyship was not pleased. She had met Wesley on his own ground with her well-disciplined troops responding to her instructions; but she had been worsted. He had been the stronger both in strategy and battle. It was not pleasant to meet an equal, but to meet one who in the art of leadership was superior was galling indeed.

Throughout the remainder of this decade Wesley had to meet a two-pronged attack. The first kind of thrust came from such bitter, envenomed controversialists as Augustus Toplady, Richard and Rowland Hill, and the authors of a succession of violent articles in the *Gospel Magazine*. The second kind of assault arose from the decision to send the preachers of the Lady Huntingdon Society not to unevangelized areas but to places where Methodism was strong; they

[25] See especially *Life of Selina Countess of Huntingdon*, II.241-2 and Luke Tyerman's *Life and Times of John Wesley*, III.93-4.

were to disrupt the societies by their attack on Wesley and his doctrines.

When Wesley came to Ormiston, ten miles south of Edinburgh, he found that a well inclined minister had changed his mind because his patron the Earl of Hopetoun had heard from Lady Huntingdon that Methodists 'were dreadful heretics to whom no quarter should be given'. Wesley with great restraint observed: 'It is a pity! Should not the children of God leave the devil to do his own work?'[26]

Similarly, in November 1776 when he came to Norwich, he found that many friends had been shaken 'by the assertors of the Horrible Decrees'. It took three whole mornings for him to sift the question to the bottom and to confirm the wavering in their faith.[27] The trouble had arisen largely because the Norwich Tabernacle had passed into the hands of Lady Huntingdon. A Calvinist, the Rev. Mark Wilks, had been appointed minister, and the pulpit was also supplied regularly by Trevecca students. It was these whom Wesley castigated as 'those vulgarly-called gospel preachers'. By August 1778 he rejoiced to find that 'peace and love prevailed throughout the circuit. Those who styled themselves My Lady's Preachers, who screamed, and wailed, and threatened to swallow us up, are vanished away.'

In other places he was not so fortunate. When he came to Grimsby on 3rd July 1779, he found that

[26] 12th May 1772, *Journal*, V.460. [27] *Journal*, VI.131.

'those striplings who call themselves Lady Huntingdon's preachers have greatly hindered the work of God'. He declared that 'they have neither sense, courage, not grace to go and beat up the devil's quarters in any place where Christ has not been named; but wherever we have entered as by storm, and gathered a few souls, often at the peril of our lives, they creep in, and by doubtful disputations, set every one's sword against his brother'. He said that one had just crept into Grimsby and was trying to divide the little flock.[28] This was the one occasion when Wesley's indignation was stronger than his contempt.

Nevertheless his strong action at the 1771 Conference and his refusal to bandy personalities with either the writers or the preachers who attacked him meant that the venomous arrows fell harmlessly to the ground. His own positive preaching and writing, and the example he offered his followers, won the final victory against the attacks of his Calvinist opponents. When the decade came to its close the rout was complete. For the last decade of his life Wesley was received everywhere with honour and profound respect. Calumny had been silenced. His own refusal to enter the cockpit with the Calvinists, and the testimony of his own life, coupled with the spoken and written expressions of his own views, had

[28] *Journal*, VI.241-2. On 20th June 1780 he reported about Grimsby 'Here is still a loving people, though a little disturbed by Calvinists who seize on every halting soul as their own lawful prey.'

THE ASTONISHING YOUTH

brought him unscathed through this last and sharpest period of controversy. Once again the leader had not been found wanting.

In the fifth decade of his public ministry, Methodism emerged not only as a separate Church rather than a Society within the Church of England, but as a world Church. It was in this period that the true dimensions of his movement became evident. The credit of publicizing Sunday-schools must be given to Robert Raikes of Gloucester, but they were actually started by Hannah Ball, the Methodist, in High Wycombe some years earlier.[29] Wesley saw their possibilities at once, and whereas before he had preached frequently to parents on the education of children, now the *Journal* recorded his meetings with the children themselves. He found them 'lively', 'affectionate', 'fair blossoms'. Writing to Richard Rodda he spoke approvingly of setting up Sunday-schools in Chester and declared that 'they would be our great means of reviving religion throughout the nation'.[30] In a letter to Duncan Wright he became still more eloquent in their praise. He believed them to be 'one of the noblest works of charity which have been set on foot in England since the time of William the Conqueror'.[31] In one last instance which might be selected from his correspondence he waxed bolder

[29] In 1783. See *John Wesley and the Eighteenth Century*, p. 136, and L. Tyerman, *Life of Wesley*, I.10.
[30] 17th January 1787.
[31] 9th January 1788; Cf. *Journal*, VII.351, note.

THE DECADES OF HIS MINISTRY

still; for in a letter to Charles Atmore he said Sunday-schools 'were one of the best institutions which have been seen in Europe for some centuries'.[32]

The older he grew the more lyrical did he become in their praise, and through his encouragement the Methodist people took a foremost lead in the instruction of the young. Within sixty years of his death there were 400,000 children being taught in Wesleyan Sunday-schools.[33] Despite his own protests, a body that was actively shepherding and instructing the young over the whole country could not be a Religious Society within the Church of England; by such generous provision for its future enlargement it was already a separate Church.

The legal acknowledgement of that fact lay in the Deed of Declaration. Signed in the office of Mr Clulow on 28th March 1784, its purpose was conveyed in its title: 'The Rev. John Wesley's Declaration and Establishment of the Conference of the People called Methodists, enrolled in his Majesty's High Court of Chancery'.[34] By its main provision the Conference through its Legal Hundred became Wesley's legal heir. Wesley was making proper provision for a Church that he knew would have an independent existence after his death.

But John Wesley in this last decade was laying the

[32] 25th March 1790. [33] *Minutes of Conference*, 1854.
[34] *Journal*, VI.481, note. The Deed is given in extenso, VIII.335-41. See also Wesley's letter to the 1785 Conference written on 7th April 1785.

foundations not only of a separate Church but of a world Church. He not only looked upon the world as his parish but he made it so. The ordinations of 1784 were the boldest, most irregular, and most completely justified actions of his long life. When after earnest endeavour he was quite unable to persuade any bishop to ordain men for the work in America, he acted upon the conviction, which had been his since reading Lord King's *Account of the Primitive Church*, that as bishops and presbyters are of the same order they have an equal right to ordain. His *Journal* entries are tense and factual.

Sept. 1st Wednesday. 4. Prayed, ordained Rd Whatcoat and T. Vasey, letters.

Thursday 2. 4. Prayed, ordained Dr Coke (as a Superintendent by the imposition of my hands, and prayer) (being assisted by other ordained Ministers).[35]

It is in his famous letter to 'Our Brethren in America' that Wesley discloses the reasons which prompted him to take so grave a step.[36] He emphasizes the fact that the 'Provinces of North America' have become independent; now 'no one exercises or claims any ecclesiastical authority at all'. He is at pains to show the difference between England where bishops have a legal jurisdiction and America where there are neither bishops nor parish ministers, 'so that for some

[35] *Journal*, VII.15 and note 2.
[36] Bristol, 10th September 1784.

hundreds of miles together there is none either to baptize or to administer the Lord's supper'.

In these desperate circumstances Wesley had no further scruples in seeing that the hungry sheep were fed. His letter to Barnabas Thomas[37] shows that he had sought the help of the Bishop of London and other bishops all in vain. He was not ready to see them deprived indefinitely of the sacraments of Baptism and the Lord's Supper, nor to have them under his own control. If the colonies were free politically, let the Methodists amongst them be free ecclesiastically. To appoint Francis Asbury (with Thomas Coke) as superintendent was to give them their own spiritual head; to prepare for them a liturgy was to recognize their own independent existence. They were no more to attempt to grow under the shadow of the Anglican Church. His letter was their charter of freedom; henceforth there was an autonomous Methodist Church of America.

Because the act of ordination surprised and scandalized his friends and most of all his own brother, John Wesley defended his conduct and motives in a statement to the Conference of 1785. But indeed no defence was necessary; he was only recognizing the logic of events. Nevertheless it required courage of a high order to set aside current ecclesiastical procedure and to brave the vehement displeasure of his friends. His act was the greatest sign of his willingness

[37] Birmingham, 25th March 1785.

to push through any obstacles so long as the needs of the Methodist people were served. The leader who had 'consented to be more vile' and to preach in the open air was driven by the inexorable demands of his work to gather his people into societies and build preaching houses, to raise an army of 'assistants' and local preachers for the succour of the flock, to organize the work into circuits and under the direction of Conference, to ordain men for work in other countries, to secure the succession of authority, and finally to license his chapels under the Act of Toleration.[38] Only a man sure of himself and unafraid of public opinion would have committed himself to such a course of action. Through such bold and adventurous leadership the world Methodist Church was born.

In the next decade Wesley lived but a year. It was sufficient to show that a man who showed such mastery in life could show it also in the presence of death. He won the respect and affection of people by the way he lived and in the end by the way he died. Indeed all the Wesleys knew how to die. When the Rector lay on his death bed he said prophetically to Charles: 'Be steady. The Christian faith will surely revive in the Kingdom: you shall see it though I shall not.' When in those last hours John asked if he was in pain, the Rector said: 'God does chasten me with pain, yea, all my hours with strong pain; but I thank

[38] 3rd November 1787, *Journal* VII.339.

him for all, I bless Him for all, I love Him for all.' John Wesley spoke of his 'serene and cheerful countenance' in the hour of dying, and recorded that 'without one struggle' he fell asleep. So too when Susanna Wesley came to die she had 'no doubt or fear'. John Wesley wrote in his *Journal:* 'She was in her last conflict; unable to speak, but I believe quite sensible. Her look was calm and serene, and her eyes fixed upward, while we commended her soul to God. . . . We stood round her bed and fulfilled her last request uttered a little before she lost her speech: "Children as soon as I am released, sing a psalm of praise to God." '[39]

It was in the high tradition of their parents that the children met death. When Kezzy died, Charles Wesley could write: 'Full of thankfulness, resignation and love, without pain or trouble she recommended her spirit into the hands of Jesus and fell asleep.'[40] When Martha was dying, she said to her niece Sally: 'I have the assurance which I have long prayed for. Shout!'

The account of Wesley's last days was written in detail by Elizabeth Ritchie, who was faithfully waiting upon him.[41] We know that on Tuesday, 1st March 1791, the day before he died, he began singing his brother's hymn:

---

[39] See also Wesley's letter to Charles, 31st July 1742, and the letter to Howell Harris, 6th August 1742; and also the *Arminian Magazine* (1787), 312.
[40] 10th March 1741.   [41] *Journal*, VIII.133-44.

THE ASTONISHING YOUTH

*All glory to God in the sky
And peace upon earth be restored.*

A little later he chose with great appropriateness to sing a hymn by Isaac Watts:

*I'll praise my Maker while I've breath;
And when my voice is lost in death,
Praise shall employ my nobler powers. . . .*

Falling back exhausted he called on his friends to 'pray and praise'. His loud Amens showed that he was joining in the intercessions of his friends.

Then he strove to speak himself, but none could understand him, so he paused a little and with all his remaining strength he cried out, 'The best of all is, God is with us', and again lifting up his arm repeated the heart-reviving words: 'The best of all is, God is with us!' Throughout the night when he tried to speak he could only whisper, 'I'll praise—I'll praise', and the last word he was heard to articulate early on the Wednesday morning, 2nd March, was 'Farewell'.

To this familiar story ought to be added the account given by James Rogers of the overwhelming impression Wesley's last hours made upon him. He said: 'The weight of glory which seemed to rest on the dying countenance of our beloved pastor, father, and friend as he entered the joy of his Lord, filled our breasts with holy dread, mixed with ineffable sweetness. God was surely in this place!'[42]

[42] *The Experience and Labours of James Rogers*; cf. *Journal*, VIII.144.

Mrs Rogers was even more graphic: 'The solemnity of the dying hour of that great, good man I believe will ever be written on my heart. . . . A cloud of the divine presence rested on all! And while he could hardly be said to be an inhabitant of earth, being now speechless, and his eyes fixed, victory and glory were written on his countenance.—Could he have spoken it would have been nothing but "Victory! victory! grace! grace! glory! glory!" '.[43]

[43] Ibid. p. 50

THE FINAL ANALYSIS

CHAPTER FIVE

THE FINAL ANALYSIS

THIS SELECTION of main happenings in the successive decades of John Wesley's ministry illustrates the strength of his personality. By his personal qualities he charmed people, but by his unrivalled powers of leadership he won a respect bordering on reverence. This dominance over the hearts and minds of people did not come through a singleminded concentration upon his evangelistic work. Though he warned his preachers that they had nothing to do but to save souls, he did not wish this dictum to be taken with severe literalness. The literature which filled their saddle-bags, the advice he gave about their studies, and his directive to them on social questions, showed how widely he interpreted their calling. He himself was the foremost social reformer of the century. Indeed it is interesting to note that when the *Gentlemen's Magazine* reported his death, the encomium was not concerned with his preaching or Church building, but with his doing 'infinite good to the lower classes of the people'. The obituary declared that 'by the humane endeavours of him and his brother Charles a sense of decency in morals and religion was introduced in the lowest classes of mankind: the ignorant were instructed, the wretched relieved, and the abandoned reclaimed'. In a striking sentence it affirmed that his private influence was greater than that of any private gentleman in the country. In similar fashion the *Monthly Review* and the *Annual Register* spoke of the extent of his labours and social influence![1]

Those who think of him, therefore, as supremely great because he was incomparable as an evangelist are casting him in too narrow a mould. This was the man who galloped up to the Newcastle Town Moor to enhearten the soldiers when Bonnie Prince Charlie was expected to come down that way into England. This was the ardent patriot who defended the Commons in its ejection of John Wilkes from his seat in Parliament,[2] and who condemned the caustic anti-Government Letters of Junius in severest terms.[3] This was the understanding politician who sought by every means in his power to avert the clash between Great Britain and the American colonies, and who in his letters to Lord North and Lord Dartmouth showed a keen appreciation of the colonists' grievances and the imminence of conflict. But this was also the loyalist who when war broke out had no doubt where his duty lay. His three pamphlets defending the action of the Government were based on legality,

---

[1] See *John Wesley and the Eighteenth Century* (1955 edn), p. 198.
[2] 'Thoughts on Liberty', *Works*, XI.41; 'Free Thoughts on Public Affairs', ibid. p. 28.
[3] 'Thoughts on Liberty', p. 44.

THE FINAL ANALYSIS

liberty, and history.[4] The administration had no more influential supporter, and 40,000 copies of his *Calm Address* were sold in the first three months—an astonishing number for a pamphlet of a purely political nature. Throughout his long life his unwavering support of 'King and Constitution' must have greatly steadied his people in days of turbulence and disaffection. It is quite untrue to say that because of Methodism, England was saved from a parallel on these shores to the French Revolution; that would never have happened. But unquestionably Wesley's strong political convictions, added to the deflection of discontent into religious channels, softened considerably the impact of the Revolution on the working classes of England.

But if Wesley was a politician, he was even more an enthusiastic and untiring social reformer. He was one of the first great Englishmen to protest against the trade in slaves.[5] More strongly than any other eminent person he attacked the popular practice of smuggling.[6] Under his instruction the Conference of 1767 addressed itself to the question of how smuggling might be abolished and gave four answers: (1) Speak tenderly and frequently of it in every Society near the coast, (2) Carefully disperse the *Word to a*

[4] *Calm Address to our American Colonies: Observations on Liberty; Calm Address to the Inhabitants of England.*
[5] See his *Thoughts on Slavery* (1774) and his letters to Granville Sharpe, 11th October 1787, and William Wilberforce, 24th February 1791.
[6] *Word to a Smuggler* (1767).

Smuggler, (3) Expel all who will not leave it off, (4) Silence every Local Preacher who defends it. A third most common practice denounced unequivocally by Wesley was bribery and corruption at election time. His *Word to a Freeholder*, written before the 1747 election, denounced every form of political corruption; he was not even willing to allow a voter to accept food or entertainment from the candidate. 'Act', he argued, 'as if the whole election depended on your vote.' Methodists became known as the most incorruptible voters in the realm. And to speak truly, who attacked more vigorously than Wesley such social evils as drinking spirituous liquor, gambling, and savage sports?

Yet John Wesley was never content with negatives. If he denounced social wrong, he was consistently advocating social righteousness. He has no place in the theory of education, but who in that century did more to promote its practice? He made a not altogether successful attempt to start Orphan Schools, but at least he provided an incentive and an example. His school at Kingswood for the sons of his preachers had its early vicissitudes, but it still remains one of the great Public Schools of England. Through his life and influence Methodism in the next century was a great pioneer in the establishment of both Day and Secondary Schools.

Wesley was greatly interested in bodily health, and as we have already pointed out, his letters contain

THE FINAL ANALYSIS

numerous references to the physical well-being of his correspondents. His book on *Primitive Physick* had run into the twenty-three editions by the time of his death. In 1746 he started to give medicine freely to the poor, and in six months some hundreds had been treated. Thus encouraged, he opened a highly successful dispensary at Bristol. In London four centres were established, and it was here that he used his electrical machine mainly for the treatment of rheumatic disorders.[7]

Lastly, we must remember Wesley's interest in the very poor.[8] Time and again he devised schemes for giving employment to the workless. He started a 'Lending Stock' to give loans to those who wanted to start in business; and Lackington, the famous bookseller, received his start from this fund. Thirdly, he gave direct encouragement to the Strangers' Friend Societies which were started in Methodism at the end of his life.[9]

John Wesley, therefore, was concerned with the whole of man. His interest was both in regeneration and reform. He had a word for the individual and for society. His mastery over men did not derive from a single gift expressing itself in a single way. It came from a richly stored mind exempting no area of life from his interest, but seeking ever to bring men and

[7] For this whole subject see Tyerman's *Life of Wesley*, I.525; Steven's *History of Methodism*, I.371; Telford's *Life*, pp. 334-5; and A. Wesley Hill's *John Wesley among the Physicians, passim*.
[8] *Journal*, 7th May 1741. [9] Benson's *Apology*, pp. 358-70.

their social conditions under the 'kind but searching glance' of God. And yet it is as an evangelistic of apostolic zeal that he is finally known. Before he died, his people, like himself, were coming to regard the world as their parish and his influence was spreading to the ends of the earth.

This was not just because of his genius in organization but because of his originality as a theologian. It is fashionable to say that Wesley was not an original thinker but derived his leading ideas from other sources and never systematized them. This, however, is not a grave criticism. The same sort of charge has been levelled at Jesus, whose leading ideas, some would maintain, were all derived from the Old Testament. But what matters is not whether a man's ideas were, in some form, in existence beforehand, but how he assembles and emphasizes them.

John Wesley was a child of the Reformation, but he gave a new pungency and direction to Reformation truth. The two great leaders, Martin Luther and Calvin, had lived in the age of Renaissance monarchy; They knew of the prince secure in his splendour and absolute in his power. Democracy as a form of government was unknown to them, and in any case to men of their temperament and outlook it would have been abhorrent. Theology has its own essential marks which are present in every age, but its emphasis is in measure shaped by the thought forms of the age in which it is expressed. Not only from their

THE FINAL ANALYSIS

reading in the Scriptures, but as children of their age, the Reformers were able to conceive of God in his sovereign majesty as high and lifted up beyond all dominion and power and might and glory. Calvin even more than Luther could stress God's selective activity whereby some for His glory are elected to be saved and others to serve His justice are reprobated to condemnation. Both spoke of God's love and both most tellingly of His mercy; nevertheless the final impression is of the King upon His throne. He moves in grace so that by our faith we become the recipients of His bounty; then indeed we know our full stature because the King's hand has been upon us for good. But we are the recipients who at all times wait on God's decisive act.

There was nothing in this august conception of God which John Wesley denied. Indeed Wesley acknowledged that he had come 'to the very edge of Calvinism' and that he accepted all but 'the horrible decrees'. No one spoke of God, high and lifted-up, with deeper reverence. When he excised some of the more affectionate language of his brother's hymns it was that nothing might even appear to dim God's glory or cheapen Him in human eyes. For that reason he even hesitated before allowing the 'dear' to stand in Charles's moving verse:

> *Come then and to my soul reveal*
> *The heights and depths of grace,*

THE ASTONISHING YOUTH

The wounds which all my sorrows heal,
That dear disfigured face.

—so great was his awe of God Almighty before whom even cherubim and seraphim veil their faces.

Yet John Wesley lived in an age which knew the stirrings of democracy. In its political philosophy it began with Locke and moved through Edmund Burke to Godwin, Priestley, and Tom Paine. The Romantic Revival in English letters was not only a renascence of wonder but a discovery of the worth of ordinary men, and this discovery rang through the accents of poets so various as Burns, Blake, Cowper, Crabbe and Wordsworth. At the Renaissance came the emergence of man: the end of the eighteenth century saw the emergence of men.

John Wesley was the child of his age. He could no longer easily think of God as the absolute Ruler when despotism was out of fashion. He made the bold and original move of recognizing the sovereignty of God but declaring it to be the sovereignty of love. The King is the Father; His power is the power of love. It is significant that on the very night of his conversion when he sang the hymn which Charles had composed two days before, it was of love and not of might he sang:

O how shall I the goodness tell,
Father, which Thou to me hast showed?

THE FINAL ANALYSIS

That I, a child of wrath and hell,
I should be called a child of God,
Should know, should feel my sins forgiven,
Blest with this antepast of heaven!

This was the dominant note of John Wesley's theology as it was of Charles Wesley's hymnody. When he preached his classic sermon on Salvation by Faith he defined it as Salvation from the guilt and fear and power of sin. God is no longer the 'Master' but the 'Father'. Christians in such a state are persuaded 'that neither death nor life, nor things present nor things to come, nor height nor depth, nor any other creature shall be able to separate them from the love of God which is in Christ Jesus our Lord'.

This same theme was that of Charles Wesley's greatest hymns on Salvation. In his 'Wrestling Jacob' there is the night-long struggle with the heavenly adversary. Jacob will not release his hold until he knows his name:

> *Wilt Thou not yet to me reveal*
> *Thy new, unutterable name?*
> *Tell me, I still beseech Thee, tell;*
> *To know it now resolved I am:*
> *Wrestling, I will not let Thee go,*
> *Till I Thy name, Thy nature know.*

When the answer is given all is given; the wrestler becomes the prevailer:

THE ASTONISHING YOUTH

> *'Tis Love! 'tis Love! Thou diedst for me!*
>   *I hear thy whisper in my heart;*
> *The morning breaks, the shadows flee,*
>   *Pure, universal Love Thou art;*
> *To me, to all, Thy mercies move:*
> *Thy nature and Thy name is Love.*

When he speaks of God's mighty act to effect our salvation Charles combines the power and the love of God:

> *Thou canst o'ercome this heart of mine,*
>   *Thou wilt victorious prove;*
> *For everlasting strength is Thine,*
>   *And everlasting love.*

But always it is a redeeming love so great that he tries in vain to capture its dimensions. It is 'amazing love', it is 'stupendous height of heavenly love', it is 'unexampled love'; in the end no adjectives will serve. He comes back to the elemental truth that God loves because it is His nature:

> *Love moved Him to die,*
> *And on this we rely;*
> *He hath loved, He hath loved us: we cannot tell why;*
> *But this we can tell,*
> *He hath loved us so well*
> *As to lay down His life to redeem us from hell.*

So great a love could not be reserved for the few:

THE FINAL ANALYSIS

Good Thou art, and good Thou dost,
Thy mercies reach to all.

The second distinctive doctrine of Methodism John Wesley defined as the 'Witness of the Spirit', commonly called Assurance. Our salvation rests upon the objective fact of our Lord's full, perfect and sufficient sacrifice, but we can have an assurance that we have passed from death unto life by the witness of God's Spirit with our own that we are the children of God. And what is that witness? John Wesley in his sermon on the subject reiterated words that he had used twenty years before: 'The Spirit of God directly witnesses to my spirit, . . . that Jesus Christ hath loved me, and given Himself for me.'

In developing this argument, John Wesley gives further scriptural warrant: 'Ye received not the spirit of bondage again unto fear; but ye received the spirit of adoption, whereby we cry, Abba, Father.'[10] In a word, we are no longer slaves but sons. This means that we are assured of His love to us and our new standing in Him. Charles Wesley set this to music. The assurance is a foretaste of that divine love which one day we shall experience perfectly.

Yet onward I haste
To the heavenly feast:
That, that is the fullness; but this is the taste;

[10] 'The Witness of the Spirit'; Romans 8:16.

THE ASTONISHING YOUTH

And this I shall prove,
Till with joy I remove
To the heaven of heavens in Jesus's love.

The third distinctive teaching of John Wesley was on that Scriptural Holiness, which is defined as Perfect Love. He declared holiness to be loving God with all our heart and soul and mind and strength, and our neighbours as ourselves. But how are we to love so unrestrainedly? We do so in response to His love for us. His love fills our heart as His Spirit fills our lives. Holiness therefore is not to be defined negatively as the striving toward sinlessness, but positively in the fulfilling of our fellowship with God. There is a perfection of the acorn, though it is not the perfection of the oak. We grow in grace, and so in holiness, as our communion with God becomes deeper and less broken. When Wesley spoke of some points of difference with the Church of England, he said 'They speak of sanctification or (holiness) as if it were an outward thing. . . . I believe it to be an inward thing, namely, the life of God in the soul of man; a participation of the divine nature.'[11]

A verse from Charles Wesley's hymn on holiness, 'God of all power and truth and grace', perfectly lights up this truth. It is much to be deplored that the verse is no longer in modern hymnbooks:

[11] *Journal*, II.275, 13th September 1739.

THE FINAL ANALYSIS

Perform the work Thou hast begun,
My inmost soul to Thee convert:
Love me, for ever love Thine own,
And sprinkle with Thy blood my heart.

But this indeed is the tenor of all his hymns on sanctification. How does it come? let him answer:

Thy nature, gracious Lord, impart;
Come quickly from above,
Write Thy new name upon my heart,
Thy new, best name of love.

Finally, John Wesley unweariedly stressed the idea of fellowship. 'The Bible', he said, 'knows nothing of solitary religion', and again 'all holiness is social holiness'. Just as he rejected politically the radical notion of a democracy that was atomistic and not organic, so he rejected theologically the notion that the Kingdom of God was but an aggregation of pardoned sinners. He never envisaged a collection, but always a society of the redeemed. In his sermon on the Catholic Spirit he is willing to accept those who practise different modes of worship as being of his own heart, providing they love God with all their heart and soul and mind and strength, and their neighbour as themselves. And this love which he shares with them and which makes him say 'Give me thy hand' is a response to God's own love. So in a magnificent peroration he can conclude: 'And now run the race which is set before thee, in the royal way of universal love. Take heed, lest thou be either wavering in thy judgement, or straitened in thy bowels: but keep an even pace, rooted in the faith once delivered to the saints, and grounded in love, in true catholic love, till thou art swallowed up in love for ever and ever!' The principle of Wesley's connexional system was that, by means of the closest bonds of organization, the strong must help the weak, since all were dependent on a loving God and the united societies were needed in the work of saving mankind.

Charles Wesley had no doubt whence the true source of fellowship came:

> *But out of all the Lord*
>   *Hath brought us by His love;*
> *And still He doth His help afford,*
>   *And hides our life above.*

The same note is struck in his invitation to join hearts and hands:

> *While we walk with God in light,*
> *God our hearts doth still unite;*
> *Dearest fellowship we prove,*
> *Fellowship in Jesu's love:*
> *Sweetly each, with each combined,*
> *In the bonds of duty joined,*
> *Feels the cleansing blood applied,*
> *Daily feels that Christ hath died.*

THE FINAL ANALYSIS

There are those who speak of the Wesley emphasis on the Holy Spirit, and indeed that is evident both in the sermons of John and the hymns of Charles. After all one cannot speak of the new birth, the witness of the Spirit, sanctification, and fellowship, without directly underlining the person and work of the Holy Spirit. Even so, the uniqueness of the Methodist contribution was in the apprehension of the almighty love of God and all this involves for the believing heart.

When one comes to a final assessment, Wesley's originality as a reformer, organizer and theologian is but his originality as a man. Through the eyes of his critics as well as his friends, he emerges as one who was immensely respected and immensely loved. His mastery over men did not prevent him from capturing their hearts. It is this combination of almost irresistible strength and charm which still makes him a man of flesh and blood and not a ghostly figure from the past.

Perhaps the best illustration of this was at the very last. In his last Will and Testament, he had directed that 'there be no hearse, no coach, no escutcheon, no pomp, except the tears of those that loved me and are following me to Abraham's bosom'. In a remarkable way these solemn injunctions were fulfilled. There was no elaborate preparation for the funeral, and the early hour of the interment was in itself an attempt to fulfil his wish for utmost simplicity. Six poor men, as directed, carried his body to the grave, but a vast multitude had already gathered. When the officiating minister, read the familiar words of committal, 'Forasmuch as it hath pleased Almighty God of His great mercy to take unto Himself the soul of our dear brother here departed', he substituted the word 'father'. The effect was instantaneous. A sudden sense of loneliness overwhelmed the mourners. They had not lost a leader; they had lost a father. Here was one they not only revered but loved. They were fatherless. A low sound of moaning and sobbing swept through them all.

Even the non-Christian, as he estimates John Wesley's work and influence during the eighteenth century, must recognize his towering stature. If he will further consider the effect of his life upon the destinies of his own country, and will reflect upon that world-wide Methodist Church which bears the marks of his genius, he may well place him in the innermost circle of the world's great leaders. Yet even this still leaves the spiritual children of John Wesley unsatisfied; for Methodists everywhere he remains, under God, the father of us all.

INDEX

Aldersgate Street, 79
Annesley, Dr Samuel, 73
Asbury, Francis, 46, 103

Beaumont, Dr, 45
Bell, George, 24, 90, 91
Bennet, John, 23f., 43
Benson, Joseph, 56, 95
Birrell, Augustine, 70
Böhler, Peter, 78f.
Burke, Edmund, 24, 118
Byrom, Dr, 48

Calvin, John, 117
Calvinist Conference (1771), 96
Cennick, John, 23f., 89
Charterhouse, 75
Crabbe, 19
Coke, Dr, 46, 56, 102
Collection of Hymns and Psalms (1737), 78
Cork Riots, 87

Deed of Declaration (1784), 46
Dictionary, Complete English, 70
Doctrines:
  Salvation, 119
  Assurance, 121
  Scriptural Holiness, 122
  Christian Fellowship, 123

Epworth Rectory, 33f.

Fletcher, John, 95f.
Franklin, Benjamin, 65
French prisoners, 88
French Revolution, 113

Gentleman's Magazine, 19, 111
Georgia, State of, 19, 76ff.

Gibson, Bishop, 25
Gospel Magazine, 96, 97

Hall, Westley, 21, 42
Hampson, John, 49
Harris, Howell, 48
Hervey, James, 21
Hill, Rowland, 29, 95
Holy Club, 20, 35, 75
Hopkey, Sophy, 76, 77
Hopper, Christopher, 56, 72
Huntingdon, Countess of, 90, 94, 95

Ingham, Benjamin, 20

Joyce, Mathias, 64

Kingswood School, 23, 114
Kirkham, Robert, 75

Lavington, Bishop of Exeter, 26
'Lending Stock', 115
Locke, John, 118
Lollards, the, 74
Luther, Martin, 79, 117

Mansfield, Lord, 46
Maxfield, Thomas, 21f., 89f.
Munchin, Joe, 85
Murray, Grace, 23, 67

Nelson, John, 23

Oglethorpe, General, 76
O'Leary, Father, 29
Orphan Schools, 114
Oxford, 76, 81

Piette, Maximin, 81

Raikes, Robert, 100
Relly, James, 21
Rodda, Richard, 100
Rogers, James, 106
Romantic Revival, the, 118

Sellon, Walter, 28
Shirley, Walter, 96f.
Smollett, William, 25
Snowsfields Chapel, 91, 92
Southey, Robert, 69
Sunday-schools, 100f.
Strangers' Friend Societies, 115

Theron and Aspasio, 20
Thompson, Martha, 63f.
Toleration, Act of, 104
Toplady, Augustus, 27, 29, 97

Walpole, Horace, 25, 94
Warburton, Bishop of Gloucester, 26f.
Wesley,
  Anne, 40
  Charles, 23, 41, 43, 66f., 117
  Emilia, 41f.
  Hetty, 36
  John, conversion, 80; death, 106; frugality, 73; humour, 70; leadership, 75; lover of fellow men, 62, 113; lover of children, 64; ordination, 103; physician, 62, 115; politician, 112; social reformer, 113; tenacity of purpose, 74
  Kezziah, 39, 105
  Martha, 42, 105
  Mary, 39
  Mrs John, 43, 67
  Samuel, Rector of Epworth, 33f.
  Samuel, 37, 38
  Susanna, 21, 36f., 105
Wesley's Chapel, 43
Wednesbury Riots, 85
Wheatley, James, 21
Whitefield, George, 23, 26, 48, 94, 95
Whitelamb, John, 39
Wilkes, John, 112
Williams, Thomas, 21

www.ingramcontent.com/pod-product-compliance
Lightning Source LLC
Chambersburg PA
CBHW050835160426
43192CB00010B/2035